Table of Contents

The photos on our front cover are courtesy of:

Southwestern Kabobs 105
   National Pork Producers Council

Wisconsin Cheese-Stuffed Burgers 87
   Wisconsin Milk Marketing Board

Grilled Vegetable Platter 56
   Lawry's Foods, Inc.

Cherry Berry Ricotta Shortcake 139
   Wisconsin Milk Marketing Board

Advisory Committee

Barbeques

PARTIES & POTLUCKS

Quick and Easy Recipes
SOUPS
SALADS
MAIN DISHES
DESSERTS

Compiled by
**Professional Home Economics Teachers
of California, Nevada, Oregon, Arizona and Utah**

Editor
Gerry Murry Henderson

Graphic Design, Typography and Production
Mike Burk Production Services, Port Townsend, WA

3/28M/062016/MBPS/BPI

Thank You!

For over thirty years **Creative Cookbook Company** has been publishing high quality cookbooks that have helped thousands of schools and organizations raise money to help continue their programs in our schools.

We owe special credit and thanks to all who contributed towards publishing our books:

Home Economics, Family and Consumer Science (FACS) Teachers of **Arizona, California, Nevada, Oregon,** and **Utah** who have contributed their best recipes. They teach foods and nutrition, as well as life-skills subjects. We are so fortunate to work with these outstanding teachers.

Grady Reed of Fullerton CA, helps teachers conduct successful sales throughout the Western U.S.

Mike Burk of Port Townsend, WA, is our creative designer who does such a wonderful job of overseeing the production and layout of our books so that they come out looking great each year

Ron Cline of Sacramento who drives long distances to make sure we give the kind of dependable service our customers expect

Alice Zumstein and her team at **Bang Printing** in Palmdale, CA, for quality printing

And a **Big Thanks** to the **students** who sell our books in the schools, and to YOU, the people who buy these books! You've helped support your local schools and some wonderful teachers with their important programs.

Sincerely,

Doug Herrema and **Doug Pierce,** owners, **Creative Cookbook Company,** Huntington Beach and Los Angeles, CA

Appetizers

Shrimp Cocktail Sauce

Makes 1 1/4 cups

- 3/4 cup chili sauce
- 2 to 4 tablespoons lemon juice
- 1 to 2 tablespoons horseradish
- 2 teaspoons Worcestershire sauce
- dash hot pepper sauce
- salt, to taste

Combine all ingredients; mix well. Add salt to taste; chill. Serve with shrimp or crab.

"I found this recipe years ago and never get tired of it."

Carol O'Keefe   **Canyon High School, Anaheim, CA**

Popcorn Salsa

Makes 5 cups

- 5 cups popcorn, freshly popped
- 1 (small) red bell pepper, seeded, blanched, finely chopped
- 2 (medium) tomatoes, peeled, finely chopped
- 4 scallions, finely chopped
- grated rind and juice of 2 limes
- 2 tablespoons fresh cilantro, chopped
- salt and freshly ground pepper, to taste
- tortilla chips

Pop the corn in an air popper. In mixing bowl, place red bell pepper, tomatoes and scallions. Stir in lime rind, juice and cilantro. Season to taste with salt and pepper. Cover and chill at least 30 minutes. Gently stir in popcorn after chilling mixture. Serve with tortilla chips for scooping.

"This good recipe was created by accident. It's a fun appetizer for parties."

Nicole Rehmann   **La Mesa Junior High School, Santa Clarita, CA**

NOTES & REMINDERS

NOTES & REMINDERS

Black-Eyed Pea & Corn Salsa

Makes 4 cups

1 (small) can sweet corn
2 cans black-eyed peas
6 Roma tomatoes, chopped
1 green pepper, chopped
6 green onions, chopped
2 tablespoons fresh parsley, chopped
1 jalapeño pepper, diced
$1/4$ teaspoon salt
$1/4$ teaspoon pepper
$1/2$ to $3/4$ cup Wishbone Italian dressing
corn chips, for dipping

Drain corn and peas; place in a medium mixing bowl. Add chopped vegetables, spices and dressing; mix well. Refrigerate until ready to serve. Serve with corn chips. NOTE: For a southwest flavor, replace the parsley with cilantro and add lime juice.

"My friend, Jean, made this for me one summer.
It's addicting on a hot summer day!"

Sheri Crouse   **Rhodes Junior High School, Mesa, AZ**

Elle's Dip

Serves 8

1 (8 ounce) package cream cheese, softened
1 can chili, with beans
1 to 1 $1/2$ cups cheese, grated
chips
salsa

Spread cream cheese on bottom of baking dish. Pour chili over cream cheese. Add grated cheese, a lot or a little. Microwave until cheese is melted. Serve with chips and salsa. NOTE: Recipe can easily be doubled or tripled.

"I was desperate once and concocted this - it's great!"

Eloise Hatfield   **Poston Junior High School, Mesa, AZ**

Blue Cheese Dip

Makes 4 cups

- 1 (8 ounce) package cream cheese, room temperature
- 1 cup Roquefort or blue cheese, crumbled (about 3.5 ounces)
- 1 cup mayonnaise
- 1 cup sour cream
- 1/2 cup onion, finely chopped
- 1/2 cup celery, finely chopped
- 2 cloves garlic, minced
- 1 teaspoon celery salt
- 1 teaspoon ground black pepper

Mix all ingredients in large bowl. Using electric mixer, beat until blended. Transfer to serving bowl, cover and chill at least 1 hour and up to 3 days.

"Even better the next day. Great with crackers or fresh vegetables."

Julie Shelburne   **Tulare Union High School, Tulare, CA**

Mexican Corn Dip

Makes 2 cups

- 2 cans white shoe peg corn
- 1 onion, chopped
- 1 jalapeño pepper, diced
- 1/2 cup mayonnaise
- 1/2 cup sour cream
- 8 ounces sharp cheddar cheese, grated
- Tortilla chips

Combine all ingredients and chill overnight. Serve with tortilla chips.

Jennifer Meskimen   **Silverado High School, Las Vegas, NV**

Clam Dip

Makes 2 1/2 cups

- 1 can minced clams
- 16 ounces Philadelphia cream cheese
- 1 tablespoon Worcestershire sauce
- 1/4 cup green onion, finely sliced
- 1/2 cup milk (or more)
- dash pepper
- Doritos corn chips or Wheat Thins crackers

Soften cream cheese and stir in remaining ingredients. If too thick, add more milk until desired consistency. Cover and chill several hours. Serve with Doritos chips or Wheat Thins.

"Our family's favorite!"

Donna Lile   **Western High School, Las Vegas, NV**

NOTES & REMINDERS

NOTES & REMINDERS

Salmon Dip

Serves 4 - 10

1 (15 ounce) can pink salmon
1 (8 ounce) container cream cheese
juice of 1 lemon
1 tablespoon prepared horseradish
3 tablespoons catsup
3 green onions, finely chopped
Assorted crackers, and/or vegetables

Clean salmon, removing bones and skin. Mix salmon with remaining ingredients (except crackers and assorted vegetables) and refrigerate until ready to serve. Serve with assorted crackers and fresh vegetables, such as celery, carrots and red pepper strips.

"I like to put this dip in a beautiful red or orange bell pepper which serves as a bowl and surround it with fresh vegetables and crackers. It's very attractive and delicious."
Judy Wasmann   **Half Moon Bay High School, Half Moon Bay, CA**

Spinach Dip

Makes 3 cups

$1/_2$ bunch fresh spinach, chopped,
    OR 1 (10 ounce) package frozen spinach, thawed
1 cup mayonnaise
2 cups sour cream
1 (8 ounce) can water chestnuts, drained, diced
2 green onions, chopped
2 teaspoons dill
2 to 3 teaspoons buttermilk ranch dressing mix
    OR $1/_2$ package Knorr Vegetable Soup mix
1 loaf sourdough bread, cut into cubes
fresh vegetables, for dipping

Clean and chop fresh spinach, or squeeze all moisture from thawed spinach. Mix spinach with mayonnaise, sour cream, water chestnuts, green onions, dill and dressing mix; chill 1 to 1 $1/_2$ hours. Stir well and serve in round sour dough loaf or in a bowl with bread, crackers or veggies on the side to dip. NOTE: The fresh spinach has a milder flavor.

"My students have demonstrated this for a favorite food demonstration and my family always enjoys this at our parties and picnics."
Ginny Milnik   **Sonora High School, Sonora, CA**

Mrs. Delap's Famous Bean Dip

Serves 12

> 1 (15.5 ounce) can S&W Chili Beans in Zesty Sauce
> 1 (8 ounce) package cream cheese, softened
> 1 cup sour cream
> 1 (4 ounce) can diced Ortega chiles
> 2 cups cheddar or jack cheese, shredded
> 2 teaspoons instant minced onions
> 1 (large) bag Fritos corn chips

Place all ingredients in a blender, except for the Fritos, in the order listed. Mix until thoroughly blended. Pour into microwavable 2 quart dish and cook on HIGH for approximately 8 to 10 minutes, stirring every 2 minutes, until all the cheese is melted. Serve with corn chips. NOTE: May also be used as a filling for burritos, or a topping for tostadas.

"My 'world famous bean dip'! Former students call and fax for the recipe. The best!"

Carole Delap   **Golden West High School, Visalia, CA**

Cheese and Chile Dip

Makes 3 cups

> 1 (8 ounce) package cream cheese, softened
> 2 tablespoons salsa
> 1 (14 ounce) can artichoke hearts, drained
> 1 cup cheddar cheese, shredded
> 1 (4 ounce) can diced green chiles, drained
> Tortilla chips, for dipping

In microwave safe bowl, place softened cream cheese. Stir in salsa. Chop drained artichoke hearts and add to cream cheese along with cheese and chile peppers; stir well. Microwave, covered, about 3 minutes on HIGH. Stir again and serve with chips.

"I was packing and realized that I hadn't mailed Doug a recipe. I made up this recipe, and decided that it was good enough to take along on our ski trip to Mammoth."

Gail Hurt Knieriem   **Estancia High School, Costa Mesa, CA**

Hot Artichoke Dip

Serves 12

> 3 (14 ounce) cans artichoke hearts
> 2 cups Parmesan cheese, freshly grated, divided
> $1/2$ cup mayonnaise
> 2 cloves garlic, minced
> zest of 1 lemon
> $1/4$ teaspoon cayenne pepper
> $1/4$ teaspoon ground pepper

Drain artichoke hearts and cut into quarters. Add 1 $1/2$ cups Parmesan cheese and remaining ingredients. Place in shallow baking dish. Top with remaining Parmesan

9

cheese. Bake at 400 degrees 10 to 20 minutes, until golden brown on top. Serve with your favorite crackers.

"Can be prepared up to 2 days in advance and refrigerated. Very convenient!"

Peg Ellington   **Yucca Valley High School, Yucca Valley, CA**

Hot Crab Dip

Makes 2 cups

> 1 (8 ounce) package cream cheese, softened
> $1/_2$ sweet onion, finely chopped
> 1 teaspoon horseradish
> 1 teaspoon dry vermouth
> 1 (6 ounce) can crab meat, drained
> $1/_4$ cup almonds, sliced
> assorted crackers

In a bowl, mix together cream cheese, onion, horseradish, vermouth and crab meat. Place in a small baking dish and top with almonds. Bake at 275 degrees for 25 minutes. Serve with your favorite crackers. NOTE: Make sure you bake and serve in the same dish.

"I'm asked over and over again for this recipe!"

Angela Croce   **Mira Mesa High School, San Diego, CA**

Easy Cheesy Salsa Dip

Makes 2 $1/_2$ cups

> 1 pound Velveeta cheese, cut into 2" cubes
> $1/_4$ cup milk
> 8 ounces salsa
> tortilla chips

Place cheese cubes in saucepan with milk over low heat. Stir until cheese is melted. Stir in salsa. Serve with tortilla chips.

"Leftover dip is great in omelets!"

Donna Adams Small   **Santana High School, Santee, CA**

Cheddar Cheese Fondue

Serves 4

$1/2$ pound cheddar cheese, shredded
1 tablespoon flour
$1/2$ cup milk
1 teaspoon Worcestershire sauce
pinch onion powder
pinch cayenne pepper
salt, to taste
$1/2$ loaf French bread, cubed
2 apples, cored, sliced

Mix shredded cheese and flour until cheese is well coated. In a saucepan over low heat, scald the milk. Stir in cheese, a little at a time, continuing to heat and stir until all cheese is melted. Add Worcestershire sauce, onion powder, cayenne and salt, to taste. Place in a fondue pot on warm. Serve with French bread cubes and fruit slices.

"This tastes like a homemade macaroni and cheese sauce. Add more if it's too thick."
Shauna Young **Jordan High School, Sandy, UT**

Hot Artichoke Dip

Makes 2 cups

8 ounces cream cheese, softened
1 cup mayonnaise
1 (14 ounce) can artichoke pieces, drained
1 cup Parmesan cheese, shredded

Mix all ingredients together. Microwave on MEDIUM-HIGH 8 to 10 minutes until hot and bubbly; or bake in oven at 350 degrees for 20 minutes. Serve with crackers or crusty bread pieces.

"This is a favorite of family and friends."
Shelly J. Wellins **Bolsa Grande High School, Garden Grove, CA**

Lighter Artichoke Dip

Serves 6 - 8

2 (14 ounce) cans artichoke hearts, drained, coarsely chopped
2 cups nonfat sour cream
1 cup Parmesan cheese, freshly grated
1 (4 ounce) can diced green chiles, drained
2 cloves garlic, minced
crackers, for dipping

Mix all ingredients together. Place in an ovenproof baking/serving dish and bake at 350 degrees for 25 to 30 minutes. Serve immediately with wholesome crackers.

Becky Oppen **Dana Hills High School, Dana Point, CA**

Sheepherder's Bread Dip
Serves 8

1 round loaf Sheepherder's bread, unsliced
1 (8 ounce) package cream cheese, softened
2 tablespoons milk
1 (2.5 ounce) jar chipped beef, chopped
2 tablespoons onion, finely minced
2 tablespoons bell pepper, minced
$1/8$ teaspoon pepper
$1/2$ cup sour cream
$1/2$ cup walnuts, chopped
1 loaf French bread, cut into chunks for dipping

Slice off top of Sheepherder's bread, save top. Hollow out loaf, saving bread for dipping. Mix together remaining ingredients, except French bread, and place inside hollowed out loaf. Bake at 250 degrees for 2 hours. Leave top off while baking. Serve warm with chunks of French bread.

"This can be made ahead of time and baked before guests arrive.
The house smells soooo good! It's a favorite of our family."

Charlotte Runyan　　　　　**Saddleback High School, Santa Ana, CA**

Chili Brie in Sourdough
Serves many

1 (1 pound) round loaf sourdough, unsliced
1 teaspoon chili powder
$1/2$ teaspoon dry ground mustard
$1/2$ teaspoon garlic powder
$1/2$ teaspoon sugar
1 (8 ounce) wheel brie
1 tablespoon butter, softened

Preheat oven to 350 degrees. Combine spices and sugar; set aside. Cut circle in top of bread and remove bread center to make room for brie. Spread butter in bread; sprinkle with 2 teaspoons spice blend. With knife, make 2" cuts around edge of bread at 1" intervals. Remove rind from brie and place in bread. Sprinkle brie with remaining spice blend. Replace top of bread. Bake on baking sheet for 20 to 30 minutes. To serve, remove bread top and break into bite sized pieces. Dip bread pieces in hot brie.

Nancy L. Earnest　　　　　**Victor Valley High School, Victorville, CA**

NOTES & REMINDERS

Artichoke Squares

Makes 6 dozen

        2 (small) onions, minced
        2 cloves garlic, minced
        2 tablespoons butter
        8 eggs, beaten
        $1/2$ cup fine bread crumbs
        $1/2$ teaspoon Tabasco sauce
        $1/2$ teaspoon pepper
        $1/2$ teaspoon oregano
        $1/2$ teaspoon salt
        4 cups cheddar cheese, grated
        2 tablespoons parsley, chopped
        1 (20 ounce) jar marinated artichoke hearts, drained, chopped

Sauté onions and garlic in butter until limp. In a bowl, beat eggs with a fork. Add bread crumbs and seasonings. Stir in cheese, parsley, artichokes and onion mixture. Pour into buttered 13" x 9" pan. Bake at 325 degrees for 30 minutes until set. Cut into 1" squares.

"Great as a hot or cold appetizer. Easy and serves many!"

Linda Hsieh   **Rowland High School, Rowland Heights, CA**

Easy Vegetable Squares

Makes 32   *Photo opposite page 33*

        2 (8 ounce) packages refrigerated crescent rolls (16 rolls)
        1 (8 ounce) package cream cheese, softened
        1 (3 ounce) package cream cheese, softened
        $1/3$ cup mayonnaise or salad dressing
        1 teaspoon dried dill weed
        1 teaspoon buttermilk salad dressing mix ($1/4$ of a 0.4 ounce package)
        3 cups desired toppings: Finely chopped broccoli, cauliflower
           or green pepper; seeded and chopped tomato
           or; thinly sliced green onion, black olives, or celery;
           or shredded carrots
        1 cup (4 ounces) Wisconsin Cheddar, Mozzarella,
           or Monterey Jack cheese, shredded

For crust, unroll crescent rolls and pat into a 15" x 10" x 2" baking pan. Bake according to package directions; cool. Meanwhile, in a small mixing bowl, stir together cream cheese, mayonnaise or salad dressing, dill weed, and salad dressing mix. Spread evenly over cooled crust. Sprinkle with desired toppings, then the shredded Cheddar, Mozzarella or Monterey Jack cheese.

Wisconsin Milk Marketing Board   **Madison, WI**

NOTES & REMINDERS

Appetizer Pie
Makes 2 cups

1 (8 ounce) package cream cheese, softened
2 tablespoons milk
1 (3 ounce) package chipped beef, finely chopped
3 tablespoons green onion, finely chopped
2 tablespoons green pepper, finely chopped
$1/2$ cup sour cream
$1/4$ cup pecans, finely chopped
assorted crackers

Blend cream cheese and milk in 1 quart mixing bowl. Add beef, green onion, and green pepper. Mix well. Stir in sour cream. Spread evenly in an 8" glass pie plate. Cover with waxed paper. Microwave on HIGH 2 minutes, 15 seconds or until mixture is hot. Let stand 2 minutes. Sprinkle with chopped nuts. Serve with assorted crackers.

"Great for parties or potluck dinners because it can be made ahead of time, then refrigerated. Be sure to add 2 minutes to cooking time if mixture is cold."

Diane Castro   **Temecula Valley High School, Temecula, CA**

Seven-Layer Dip
Serves 8

1 (large) can refried beans
2 ripe avocados, mashed
1 teaspoon lemon juice
1 teaspoon lemon pepper
$1/4$ teaspoon garlic salt
$1 1/2$ tablespoons salsa
1 cup + 2 teaspoons sour cream, divided
$1/2$ cup mayonnaise
$1/4$ package taco seasoning
2 cups sharp cheddar cheese, shredded
2 tomatoes, diced
1 (small) can olives, sliced
2 green onions, chopped
tortilla chips

Spread refried beans over bottom of a large platter. Combine mashed avocado with lemon juice, lemon pepper, garlic salt, salsa and 2 teaspoons sour cream; spread over beans. Mix together 1 cup sour cream with mayonnaise and taco seasoning; spread over avocado layer. Sprinkle with cheddar cheese, diced tomatoes, olives and onions. Serve with tortilla chips

"Everyone loves this one!! Perfect for parties and snack time!"

Brenda Rhodes   **West High School, Salt Lake City, UT**

Christina's Cheese Ball

Serves 10 +

- 2 packages Buddig Beef, thin sliced
- 4 (8 ounce) packages cream cheese, softened
- 2 bunches green onions, chopped
- Assorted crackers

Chop one package beef. Slice the second package into strips and set aside. Mix with cream cheese and onion. Form into a ball and cover with strips of second package of beef. Chill at least 12 hours before serving. Serve with your favorite crackers.

"Our new secretary brought this to school. We served it at my daughter's wedding".

Carole Call　　　　　　　**Costa Mesa High School, Costa Mesa, CA**

Festive Cheese Ball

Makes 1 large ball

- 2 (8 ounce) packages cream cheese, softened
- 1 (small) can crushed pineapple, drained
- 1 (small) jar pimiento, diced
- $1/4$ bell pepper, chopped
- $1/2$ carrot, peeled, grated
- 4 stalks green onion, chopped
- Lawry's Seasoned Salt, to taste
- $1/2$ cup almonds, sliced

Mix together first seven ingredients. Shape into a ball; chill. Roll in sliced almonds to cover. Chill until ready to serve.

"Serve with a variety of crackers or bagels."

Bonnie Landin　　　　　　**Garden Grove High School, Garden Grove, CA**

Cheese & Chile Roll

Serves 6 - 8

- 8 ounces Velveeta cheese, room temperature
- 2 (3 ounce) packages cream cheese, room temperature
- 1 (3 ounce) can Ortega chiles, diced
- Saltine crackers or sturdy tortilla chips, for serving

Place Velveeta cheese between two pieces of waxed paper and roll to a rectangle about 10" x 14". Carefully pull off top of waxed paper. Spread softened cream cheese over rolled out Velveeta. Spread Ortega chiles over cream cheese. Starting with long 14" side, roll up jelly roll fashion, rolling tightly and using waxed paper to help roll. Refrigerate 2 to 3 hours. Serve with crackers or tortilla chips.

"This recipe has to be the easiest to prepare."

Carla Escola　　　　　　　**Sierra High School, Manteca, CA**

NOTES & REMINDERS

Cheese Spread

Makes 1 1/4 cups

> 1 cup sharp cheddar cheese, shredded
> 1 egg, hard cooked, peeled, chopped
> 1/4 cup dill pickle, minced
> 2 tablespoons green pepper, minced
> 1 tablespoon onion, minced
> 1 tablespoon pimiento, chopped
> 2 tablespoons mayonnaise
> assorted crackers

Combine cheese, egg, dill pickle, green pepper, onion and pimiento; stir in mayonnaise. Form into a ball; chill at least 2 hours. Serve with crackers.

"This recipe is also delicious used as a sandwich spread."

Cheri Schuette   Valley View Middle School, Simi Valley, CA

Crab & Shrimp Spread

Makes 1 quart

> 2 green onions, finely chopped
> 1 (7 ounce) can crab meat, chopped
> 1 (7 ounce) can baby shrimp, chopped
> 1 cup celery, finely chopped
> 1 cup mayonnaise
> 1 can cream of mushroom soup
> 1 package Knox gelatin
> 6 ounces cream cheese, softened, cubed
> assorted crackers

Chop first four ingredients very fine and mix with mayonnaise. Heat soup (undiluted) just until boiling (do not boil). Stir gelatin into soup and keep stirring until a soupy consistency is achieved. Add cream cheese. Use a wire whisk to make smooth. Remove from heat and add mayonnaise mixture. Mix well. Pour into 1 quart casserole dish that has been rubbed with mayonnaise. Put in freezer for about 1 hour. Remove when firm. Keep refrigerated. Serve with assorted crackers.

"Our family and friends enjoy this at every get together!"

Nancy Patten   Placerita Junior High School, Newhall, CA

Samosas (East Indian Snack)

Makes 10

    3 (medium) potatoes
    $1/4$ cup peas
    1 tablespoon oil, for stir-frying
    1 teaspoon cumin
    1 $1/2$ teaspoons salt
    $1/2$ teaspoon chili powder (optional)
    1 teaspoon curry powder (optional)
    2 teaspoons cilantro, chopped (optional)
    5 cups oil, for frying
    2 tablespoons flour
    3 tablespoons water
    5 wheat flour tortillas
    Tamarind sauce or catsup, for dipping

Boil and mash potatoes. Stir fry peas in 1 tablespoon oil; add mashed potatoes and all spices. On the side, heat approximately 5 cups oil in a skillet for deep frying. Mix flour and water together to make a paste. Warm one tortilla in a skillet or frying pan and cut it in half. Shape the half tortilla in a cone shape and use the paste to seal it. Put the potato stuffing in the cone and seal the top with the paste. Repeat the same process with remaining tortillas and deep fry them in hot oil. Serve hot with tamarind sauce or catsup. NOTE: Instead of frying, Samosas could also be baked at 375 degrees for 20 minutes and broiled for about 3 minutes. Cooked meat or vegetables, finely chopped, could also be added to the stuffing.

"This is a very popular snack or appetizer in India. My students absolutely love it!"
Khushwinder Kaur   **Morada Middle School, Stockton, CA**

Stuffed Grape Leaves (Dolmathes)

Serves 20

    1 pound ground lamb
    1 pound ground turkey
    2 cups instant rice
    1 tablespoon dried mint
    2 eggs, beaten
    salt and pepper, to taste
    1 jar grape leaves
    1 can chicken stock, divided
    1 soup can water, divided
Avgolemono Sauce:
    juice from 1 lemon
    3 eggs, beaten

In large bowl, combine lamb, turkey, rice, mint, eggs, salt and pepper. Wash and drain grape leaves. Put grape leaves stem side up on work surface. Put dollop of meat/rice mixture on stem end of leaf. Fold up stem, then fold up sides over mixture and roll up like an egg roll. Place seam side down in large saucepan, layering as you go. Pour

½ can chicken broth and ½ can water over rolls. Place plate on top of rolls to hold them down, then place saucepan lid on and steam for 1 hour. Prepare Avgolemono sauce just before serving: Warm remaining ½ can chicken broth with ½ can water and slowly add juice from lemon. Very slowly add beaten eggs and stir until frothy and thickened.

"From three generations of the Vlahos family. A traditional Greek spring delicacy. Made when lamb is plentiful and grape leaves are tender. Ground turkey is added to cut the strong flavor of the lamb."

Mary Springhorn   **Anderson High School, Anderson, CA**

Baked Cheese and Olive Balls

Serves 8

    2 cups cheddar cheese, grated
    I cup flour
    I teaspoon paprika
    I cube butter, softened
    I jar green olives

Preheat oven to 400 degrees. Place cheese, flour, paprika and butter into a large bowl. Cut in butter with a pastry blender. Form dough into small balls. Press an olive into dough balls and cover completely with dough. Place olive balls on a cookie sheet. Bake 15 minutes; serve hot.

"These are very good to serve at a party."

Pat Smith   **Kern Valley High School, Lake Isabella, CA**

Barbara's Baked Blue Cheese Balls

Makes 32

    6 tablespoons butter
    I can Pillsbury refrigerated biscuits
    I (small) package blue cheese crumbles

Heat oven per biscuit package instructions. While oven is preheating, melt butter in baking pan. Cut biscuits into quarters. Place each quarter into baking dish with melted butter. Place at least 1" apart, as biscuits will expand while baking. Top each biscuit with a small amount of crumbled blue cheese. Bake, according to package time and temperature.

"This is a favorite, from my great aunt, Barbara Brown."

Deanna Lee   **Marina High School, Huntington Beach, CA**

Stuffed Mushrooms

Serves 12

12 fresh mushrooms
$1/2$ cup low fat cottage cheese
$1/2$ teaspoon onion powder
$1/8$ teaspoon celery salt
$1/8$ teaspoon ground mustard
dash hot pepper sauce
dash Worcestershire sauce
chopped chives or pimiento strips, for garnish

Wash mushrooms; drain. Gently wiggle stems to loosen and remove. Dry the drained mushrooms. (If stem holes are small or the entire stem did not come out, use a serrated spoon to carefully make holes larger.) Combine cottage cheese, onion powder, celery salt, ground mustard, hot pepper sauce and Worcestershire sauce in blender jar. Blend until smooth. Fill mushroom caps with cottage cheese mixture. Sprinkle with chopped chives or place pimiento strip on top of each mushroom. NOTE: The cottage cheese filling can also be used to fill celery sticks or use as a dip for raw vegetables.

"Quick and easy. Perfect for parties and potlucks!"

Melissa Webb　　　　　　　　**Lakewood High School, Lakewood, CA**

Cheese Stuffed Mushrooms

Makes 24

24 mushrooms
2 tablespoons shallots, minced
2 tablespoons margarine
1 container Rondele spread or Artichoke/Parmesan dip
nonstick cooking spray
2 tablespoons Parmesan cheese, grated

Snap stems from mushrooms and mince. Wipe mushroom caps with a damp paper towel. Sauté stems and shallots with margarine until tender. Transfer to a mixing bowl and stir in spread or dip. Meanwhile, arrange mushroom caps upside down on a baking sheet that has been sprayed with nonstick cooking spray. Broil 5 minutes or until tender. Turn caps right side up. Spoon filling into caps, mounding slightly. Top with Parmesan cheese and broil an additional 5 minutes, or until heated through.

NOTES & REMINDERS

Crab- Stuffed Mushrooms

Serves 4

12 (large) fresh mushrooms, trim tips of stems
1 $\frac{1}{3}$ tablespoons butter, divided
$\frac{1}{2}$ cup crab meat
$\frac{1}{4}$ cup celery, finely chopped
2 tablespoons mayonnaise
1 teaspoon lemon juice
dash salt
2 tablespoons fine dry bread crumbs
Garnish: Strips of pimiento, parsley sprigs

Wash mushrooms; remove caps and finely chop stems. Cook chopped stems in 1 tablespoon butter until tender but not browned. Add crab and all other ingredients except bread crumbs. Stuff caps with mixture and sprinkle tops with bread crumbs that have been combined with remaining melted butter. Broil 6" from heat about 10 minutes. Trim each with a bit of pimiento or sprig of parsley. Serve hot.

"Broiled stuffed mushrooms are a unique hot appetizer that guests will relish. Top with various garnishes and you can even be creative with your stuffing."

Donna Fippin   **Bret Harte High School, Altaville, CA**

Marinated Mushrooms

Serves 4 - 6

$\frac{3}{4}$ cup oil
$\frac{1}{4}$ cup wine vinegar
$\frac{1}{2}$ cup Worcestershire sauce
$\frac{1}{2}$ teaspoon dry mustard
5 cloves garlic
1 teaspoon salt
1 $\frac{1}{2}$ teaspoons sugar
$\frac{1}{4}$ teaspoon pepper
$\frac{1}{2}$ teaspoon paprika
1 (12 to 18 ounce) can button mushrooms
OR 1 pound (large) fresh mushrooms, cut into fourths, blanched

Mix together all ingredients and marinate in refrigerator about 24 hours.

"I got this recipe from an excellent cook and home economist, Jeanne Escalera. When I serve it, I am often asked for a copy of the recipe."

Doris L. Oitzman   **Victor Valley High School, Victorville, CA**

Crockpot Mushrooms

Serves 6 - 8

    4 cubes beef bouillon
    4 cubes chicken bouillon
    2 cups boiling water
    4 pounds fresh button mushrooms
    1 teaspoon dill seed
    1 tablespoon Accent
    1 teaspoon garlic powder
    1 1/2 tablespoons Worcestershire sauce
    1 teaspoon pepper
    1 pound butter or margarine
    1 quart water or burgundy wine

Dissolve bouillon cubes in boiling water. Add to remaining ingredients and place in crockpot. Bring ingredients to a boil on highest setting on crockpot, or bring to a boil on stove and then place in crockpot. Turn to low setting and allow to cook for at least 6 to 7 hours. The mushrooms will shrink in size causing liquid to increase but do not add more mushrooms. NOTE: Mushrooms may stay in crockpot up to 10 hours. Leaving them in any longer will cause them to be soggy.

"From my sister-in-law. I never serve it without receiving requests for the recipe."

Karol A. Meryhew   **Granger High School, West Valley City, UT**

Deviled Eggs

Makes 20

    10 eggs, hard cooked
    1/4 cup mayonnaise
    2 tablespoons butter, melted
    1 tablespoon dill, chopped
    1/4 teaspoon salt
    dash pepper

Hard cook eggs: Place room temperature eggs in pan; cover with water. Bring to a boil, reduce heat to simmer and cook for 17 minutes. Immediately remove from heat and place in cold water. Peel eggs and cut in half lengthwise. Put yolks in food processor and finely chop. Add remaining ingredients and blend until smooth. Put yolk mixture in pastry bag fitted with a large star tip and fill each half of egg. Cover loosely with plastic wrap and refrigerate up to 3 hours.

Cheryl Clubb   **Saddleback High School, Santa Ana, CA**

NOTES & REMINDERS

Stuffed Egg Halves

Serves 6

> 3 eggs, hard cooked, peeled
> 3 tablespoons mayonnaise
> 1 teaspoon Dijon mustard
> 1 teaspoon capers, chopped
> whole capers, for garnish

Carefully cut eggs in half lengthwise. Remove yolks and mash with fork in small bowl. Add mayonnaise, mustard and chopped capers. Blend together well. Spoon mixture into egg halves and top each half with a whole caper. Make several hours ahead and chill, covered.

"Easy and a little different version of an old favorite."

Linda Robinson   **Royal High School, Simi Valley, CA**

Family Favorite Wings

Makes 24 - 30

> 12 to 15 chicken wings
> 1 cup soy sauce
> 1 cup brown sugar, firmly packed
> $^1/_2$ cup butter or margarine
> 1 teaspoon dry mustard
> $^3/_4$ cup water

Disjoint chicken wings, discarding bony tips. Arrange wing parts in shallow baking pan. Combine soy sauce, brown sugar, butter, mustard and water. Heat until sugar dissolves and butter melts. Cool, then pour over wings. Marinate in refrigerator 2 hours, turning occasionally. Bake, in marinade, at 350 degrees for 45 minutes. Turn once, spoon marinade over wings occasionally. Drain on paper towels. Serve warm or cold.

"We never have a family get together without serving this tasty appetizer."

Peggie Goyak   **Birmingham High School, Van Nuys, CA**

Tangy Sweet Chicken Wings

Serves 4

> 1 pound chicken wing drumettes
> 1 package French onion soup mix
> 8 ounces Russian salad dressing
> 12 ounces apricot preserves

Line a 9" x 13" pan with foil. Spread wings in bottom of pan. In a saucepan, stir together soup mix, dressing and preserves; bring to a boil, stirring constantly. Reduce heat and simmer sauce 5 minutes. Pour over chicken. Do not cover. Bake 1 hour at 350 degrees.

"You can also grill chicken and use the sauce like a barbecue sauce."

Karyn Lanham   **Cimarron-Memorial High School, Las Vegas, NV**

Lowfat Chicken Strips

Serves 4

>2 boneless, skinless chicken breast halves
>1/4 cup flour
>1 tablespoon parsley, chopped
>1/4 teaspoon salt
>1/4 teaspoon pepper
>pinch cayenne pepper
>1 tablespoon vegetable oil
>barbecue sauce or ranch style dressing, for dipping

Cut chicken across the grain into 1/2" strips. In a bowl, combine the flour, parsley, salt, pepper and cayenne. Add the chicken strips and coat lightly. In a skillet, warm the oil over medium heat until hot, not smoking. Add chicken strips and cook, turning frequently until thoroughly cooked. Drain on paper towels. Serve as an appetizer with barbecue sauce or ranch dressing.

"This is a great snack or main dish."

Sherri Buchanan **Villa Park High School, Villa Park, CA**

Banana, Orange & Strawberry Fruit Smoothie

Serves 4

>4 fresh sweet oranges OR enough for at least 1 cup of orange juice
>1/2 banana
>1 cup strawberries, frozen

Squeeze the oranges with an electric juicer. Add the orange juice, sliced banana and frozen strawberries to a blender. Blend until mixture is smooth.
NOTE: If fresh fruit is used, add ice cubes until you have the desired thickness.

"Add your favorite fruits, such as mangos, pineapple, peaches, to suit your own taste."

Audrey Birch **Parras Middle School, Redondo Beach, CA**

The Palladium Cooler

Serves 14

>6 cups orange juice
>6 cups pineapple juice
>3 cups cranberry juice
>1 tablespoon grenadine
>1 cup 7-Up
>6 cups ice cubes
>*Garnish:* 14 maraschino cherries

Mix all ingredients together, except 7-Up and ice, in a punch bowl. Float 7-Up on top. Add ice cubes and garnish with a cherry in each cup.

"This nonalcoholic drink is served to young people, ages 16 to 21,
at New York's hottest night club, the Palladium, formerly a 1926 opera house."

Alice Claiborne **Fairfield High School, Fairfield, CA**

NOTES & REMINDERS

Lime Cream Party Punch

Makes 1 gallon

    1 quart vanilla ice cream, slightly softened
    1 quart lime sherbet, slightly softened
    1 quart milk
    6 ounces frozen lemonade concentrate
    6 ounces frozen limeade concentrate
    2 cups water
    1 quart ginger ale

In large punch bowl, stir together ice cream, sherbet and milk. In 1 quart pitcher, stir together lemonade concentrate, limeade concentrate and 2 cups water. Pour over ice cream mixture. Add ginger ale and stir until slightly mixed.

"A creamy, refreshing punch that goes well with barbecued meals."

Nan Paul　　　　　　　　　　　　　　　**Grant Middle School, Escondido, CA**

Party Punch

Serves 50

    2 cups sugar
    4 cups water, divided
    1 (6 ounce) can frozen lemonade concentrate
    2 (46 ounce) cans pineapple juice
    1 teaspoon almond extract
    3 quarts ginger ale
    orange, limes, star fruit, sliced

Dissolve sugar in 2 cups water. Add lemonade concentrate, pineapple juice, almond extract and remaining 2 cups water. Arrange sliced fruit in bottom of molds (ring molds work well). Pour in liquid and freeze. Thaw until mushy; pour ginger ale over iced fruit juices.

"Champagne may be used instead of ginger ale.
This was a hit at several baby showers I've hosted."

Charlene Nugent　　　　　　　**Petaluma Junior High School, Petaluma, CA**

Salads & Soups

Craisin Salad

Serves 18

- 1 head red leaf lettuce
- 1 head green leaf lettuce
- 1 head iceberg lettuce
- 8 ounces mozzarella cheese, shredded
- 1 (small) package Parmesan cheese, shredded
- 1 cup craisins
- 1 pound bacon, cooked, crumbled
- 1 package almonds, sliced
- 6 chicken breast halves, cooked, diced
- $1/2$ cup sweet onion, chopped
- 1 cup sugar
- 2 teaspoons dry mustard
- $1/2$ cup red wine vinegar
- 1 cup canola oil

Wash all lettuce well, break into bite-sized pieces. Toss in cheese, craisins, bacon, almonds and chicken. In a blender, combine onion, sugar, mustard, red wine vinegar; blend, slowly adding canola oil until well mixed. Toss salad and dressing together or serve dressing on the side.

Cheryl M. Moyle   **Olympus High School, Salt Lake City, UT**

Night Before Lettuce Salad

Serves 8

- 1 head iceberg lettuce
- 1 can water chestnuts, sliced, drained
- 2 ribs celery, chopped
- 1 bunch green onion, chopped
- 1 (12 ounce) package peas, frozen
- 1 cup mayonnaise
- 2 tablespoons sugar
- 12 ounces mozzarella cheese, grated

Tear lettuce and place in bottom of flat bowl or platter. On top of lettuce, layer each of the following: Water chestnuts, chopped celery, green onion, peas. Cover with mayonnaise and sprinkle with sugar. Add a layer of grated mozzarella and cover with plastic wrap or foil. Keep in refrigerator 24 hours before serving. Toss before serving.

Monica Blanchette   **Landmark Middle School, Moreno Valley, CA**

Spinach Salad

Serves 15 - 20

Dressing:

1 $^1/_2$ teaspoons poppy seeds
$^3/_4$ cup white vinegar
1 $^1/_3$ cups oil
$^3/_4$ cup sugar
1 $^1/_2$ teaspoons salt
1 $^1/_2$ tablespoons red onion, grated
$^3/_4$ teaspoon dry mustard
1 package spinach, washed, trimmed
1 (small) head iceberg lettuce, washed, torn
$^3/_4$ cup Swiss cheese, shredded
1 cup cottage cheese, rinsed, drained
$^1/_2$ cup bacon, cooked crisp, chopped
1 red onion, sliced

Combine dressing ingredients the night before serving so flavors can meld. Next day, in large salad bowl, combine spinach, iceberg lettuce, Swiss cheese, cottage cheese, bacon and sliced onion. Toss with dressing just before serving.

"Always a crowd pleaser!"

Patsy Graves   Bingham High School, So. Jordan, UT

A Different Spinach Salad

Serves 12 - 16

1 head Napa cabbage, chopped
1 bag baby spinach, washed
1 (medium) jicama, peeled, diced
1 red bell pepper, thinly sliced
brown sugar
butter
1 cup almonds, slivered
1 bag raisins
1 bottle poppy seed dressing

Add finely chopped cabbage to spinach. Toss in jicama and red pepper strips. Brown slivered almonds in brown sugar and butter. Add to salad, along with raisins. Toss well. Just before serving, toss with poppy seed dressing.

"A delightful salad with a variety of color and textures."

Paulette Evans   Cyprus High School, Magna, UT

Strawberry Spinach Salad

Serves 8

Salad:
1 bag baby spinach leaves
1 pint fresh strawberries, sliced
1 avocado, peeled, diced
1 package slivered almonds
4 tablespoons sugar

Dressing:
$1/2$ cup sugar
2 tablespoons sesame seeds
1 tablespoon poppy seeds
$1/2$ cup vegetable oil
$1/4$ cup sweet rice wine vinegar
$1/4$ teaspoon paprika
$1/4$ teaspoon Worcestershire sauce
1 $1/2$ tablespoons onion, finely chopped

Arrange spinach leaves, strawberries and avocado in bowl. In skillet, caramelize almonds by cooking in fry pan with 4 tablespoons sugar until sugar melts and coats almonds. Cool and stir. Sprinkle over salad. Combine all dressing ingredients in separate bowl and add just before serving.

"A favorite with the 'Drew Circle Barbecue Group' for its taste and its color."

Joanne Montoy   **Esperanza High School, Anaheim, CA**

Black Bean, Corn & Pepper Salad

Serves 6 - 8

2 (15 ounce) cans black beans, drained, rinsed
1 (10 ounce) package frozen corn, thawed
1 (large) red bell pepper, stemmed, seeded, diced
$1/2$ cup fresh cilantro, firmly packed, chopped
$1/4$ cup lime juice
2 tablespoons salad oil
salt and pepper, to taste
2 (small) fresh jalapeño chiles, stemmed, seeded, minced (optional)
Lettuce leaves, rinsed and crisped

In a bowl, mix beans with corn, bell pepper, cilantro, lime juice, oil, and salt and pepper to taste. Stir in chiles, if using. Cover and chill 1 hour or up until the next day. Pour into bowl lined with lettuce leaves.

"This is so good! Credit to Maria Montemagni. I am lucky to be working with someone who is kind, professional, and totally dedicated to the students!"

Brenda Burke   **Mt. Whitney High School, Visalia, CA**

NOTES & REMINDERS

27

Broccoli-Cashew-Cabbage Salad

Serves 8

2 pounds broccoli florets, bite-sized
1 (very small) head cauliflower, trimmed, to bite size
3 to 4 cups red cabbage, thinly sliced
1 can salted cashew halves
2 cups mayonnaise
3 tablespoons sugar
1 tablespoon white wine vinegar
$1/2$ teaspoon salt

In large bowl, combine broccoli with cauliflower, cabbage and cashews. In smaller bowl, combine mayonnaise with sugar, vinegar and salt. Toss dressing with salad and chill 2 hours.

"A delicious way to get more broccoli into your diet.
You'll get many requests for this recipe!"

Carol Goddard   **Alhambra High School, Alhambra, CA**

Cranberry Walnut Cole Slaw

Serves 8 - 10

$1/4$ cup mayonnaise
1 tablespoon sweet pickle relish
1 tablespoon honey mustard
1 tablespoon honey
$1/4$ teaspoon ground pepper
$1/8$ teaspoon salt
$1/8$ teaspoon celery seed
5 cups green cabbage, shredded
$1/3$ cup walnuts, chopped
$1/4$ cup celery, chopped
$1/4$ cup onion, finely chopped
$1/4$ cup red bell pepper, finely chopped
$1/4$ cup dried cranberries

In a small bowl, stir together mayonnaise, relish, honey mustard, honey, ground pepper, salt and celery seed. In a large mixing bowl, combine cabbage, walnuts, celery, onion, red pepper and cranberries. Add dressing to cabbage mixture and toss to coat. Cover and chill at least 1 hour or up to 6 hours.

"Tasty alternative to traditional cole slaw. Cranberries and walnuts add nice color and texture to this salad. My family loves this on a hot summer day."

Teresa Hayes   **Buena High School, Ventura, CA**

Jicama-Cilantro Slaw

Serves 6

 $^1/_4$ cup salad oil
 $^1/_4$ cup lime juice
 2 tablespoons cilantro, snipped
 1 tablespoon sugar
 $^1/_4$ teaspoon salt
 $^1/_8$ teaspoon ground red pepper
 3 cups (total) green and red cabbage and carrots, shredded
 1 pound jicama, peeled, cut into thin strips
 2 green onions, thinly sliced

In a large bowl, stir together oil, lime juice, cilantro, sugar, salt and red pepper. Stir until sugar dissolves. Add cabbage, carrots, jicama and green onions; toss to coat. Cover and chill from 3 to 24 hours. Toss once more before serving and garnish with additional cilantro sprigs, if desired.

"Use a food processor to shred carrots, green and red cabbage; or use packaged shredded coleslaw vegetables."

Marguerite Smith   **Murrieta Valley High School, Murrieta, CA**

Texas Two-Step Slaw

Serves 8   *Photo opposite page 32*

 4 cups green cabbage, shredded
 1 cup red cabbage, shredded
 $^1/_4$ cup red onion, chopped
 2 jalapeño chiles, seeded, finely chopped
 2 tablespoons fresh cilantro, chopped
 1 (11 ounce) can Green Giant Mexicorn Whole Kernel Corn, Red & Green Peppers, drained
 4 ounces (1 cup) cheddar cheese, shredded
 fresh cilantro sprigs
Dressing:
 $^3/_4$ cup prepared ranch salad dressing
 1 tablespoon fresh lime juice
 1 teaspoon cumin

In large bowl, combine all salad ingredients, except cilantro sprigs; mix well. In small bowl, combine all dressing ingredients; blend well. Pour over salad; toss to coat. Serve immediately or refrigerate until serving time. Garnish with cilantro. NOTE: When handling jalapeño chiles, wear plastic or rubber gloves to protect hands. Do not touch face or eyes.

Pillsbury Company   **Minneapolis, MN**

Tomato, Cornbread & Cilantro Salad

Serves 4

1 package Jiffy corn bread, prepared according to package directions
$1/4$ cup vinegar
$1/4$ cup lime juice
3 tablespoons cilantro, minced
1 tablespoon Dijon mustard
salt and pepper, to taste
$1/4$ cup canola oil
4 plum tomatoes, chopped
4 green onions, chopped
$1/2$ cup cilantro leaves, loosely packed
1 package baby lettuce, spring mix

Whisk together vinegar, lime juice, 3 tablespoons minced cilantro, mustard, salt and pepper and oil. In large bowl, combine crumbled cornbread, tomatoes, green onion, lettuce and cilantro leaves. Stir gently to combine. Toss with vinaigrette and serve.

"My sister made this for a potluck and received raves and requests for the recipe!"
Reiko Ikkanda   **So. Pasadena Middle School, So. Pasadena, CA**

Cranberry-Broccoli Salad

Serves 6

$1/2$ cup pine nuts, toasted
1 $1/2$ cups broccoli, finely chopped
1 (small) can crushed pineapple, drained
$3/4$ cup dried cranberries
$1/2$ cup red onion, finely chopped
$1/2$ cup carrots, grated
$1/2$ cup low fat mayonnaise
$1/3$ cup white rice vinegar
$1/2$ teaspoon salt
3 tablespoons sugar

Toast pine nuts in 400 degree oven for 10 to 12 minutes; cool. Combine all ingredients in large bowl. Taste for seasoning and adjust, if desired. Chill several hours or prepare a day ahead. Keeps well in refrigerator.

Donna Young   **Santa Maria High School, Santa Maria, CA**

NOTES & REMINDERS

Broccoli Salad

Serves 4 - 8

3 tablespoons sugar
2 tablespoons red wine vinegar
$3/4$ cup mayonnaise
3 cups broccoli florets
1 cup mushrooms, sliced
$1/2$ cup red onion, chopped
$3/4$ cup raisins
6 slices bacon, cooked crisp, crumbled
$1/2$ cup almonds, sliced

Combine sugar with vinegar and mayonnaise. Toss with broccoli, mushrooms and onions; allow to marinate 1 hour. Add raisins, bacon and almonds; toss gently and serve.

"Delicious! Always a hit and a favorite for pot lucks. Easy to double the recipe too!"

Debra Purcell   **Cope Middle School, Redlands, CA**

Artichoke Salad

Serves 4 - 6

1 (14 ounce) can artichoke hearts, quartered, drained
1 (6 ounce) jar marinated artichoke hearts
1 (3 ounce) can mushrooms, sliced
1 (small) sweet onion, finely chopped
$1/2$ cup roasted red pepper, sliced $1/4$" thick
$1/4$ teaspoon Dijon mustard
$1/4$ cup olive oil
2 tablespoons red wine vinegar
salt and pepper, to taste

In a serving bowl, combine all ingredients and toss. Chill well before serving.

Angela Croce   **Mira Mesa High School, San Diego, CA**

Fennel and Radish Salad

Serves 4 - 6

1 $1/2$ pounds fennel bulbs
2 bunches (about 30) red radishes
$1/2$ cup olive oil
3 tablespoons wine vinegar
$1/2$ teaspoon salt
freshly ground pepper
2 tablespoons parsley, chopped
Lettuce leaves or Belgian endive leaves

Trim the fennel and slice it very thin. Trim the radishes (don't peel them) and shred them in a food processor, using shredding disk. Toss the fennel and radishes

NOTES & REMINDERS

31

together. In a tightly capped jar, shake together the oil, vinegar, salt and pepper. Pour over vegetables and toss to combine flavors. Let marinate 1 to 2 hours, tossing occasionally. Just before serving, toss in parsley and mound the salad on lettuce or endive leaves. NOTE: Fennel season runs from fall to early spring. For another version, toss raw fennel slices with orange slices, red onion slices and black olives. Dress the salad with olive oil and lemon juice!

"This cool, crunchy salad with a delicate anise flavor and shreds of red radish, is best eaten within a few hours. If refrigerated overnight, it becomes more of a relish!"

Janet Tingley   **Atascadero High School, Atascadero, CA**

Kay Kay's Chicken Salad

Serves 4 - 6

$1/2$ cup almonds, slivered
2 tablespoons sesame seeds
1 package Top Ramen noodles, plus dry mix, divided
2 tablespoons sugar
3 tablespoons white vinegar
$1/4$ cup water
$1/4$ cup salad oil
1 teaspoon salt
$1/2$ head cabbage, chopped
4 green onions, thinly sliced
1 red bell pepper, chopped
2 cups chicken breast, cooked, shredded or diced
cilantro, chopped (optional)

Toast almonds with sesame seeds; cool. Break Top Ramen noodles into pieces and add to almonds and sesame seeds; set aside. In a small bowl, combine sugar, vinegar, water, salad oil, salt and $1/2$ package Top Ramen noodle dry mix. Blend well; set aside. In a large bowl mix together cabbage, green onions, red pepper, chicken and cilantro, if desired. Combine all ingredients and toss just before serving.

"Recipe may be easily doubled. Dressing is delicious so make enough. Most things can easily be done ahead of serving time. Salad is tasty the next day so make a lot."

Diane Wolak   **Martin Luther King High School, Riverside, CA**

Texas
Two-Step Slaw
SALADS.....PAGE 29

Chicken Curry Salad

Serves 6

2 cups boiling water
1 package dry chicken noodle soup mix
1 cup instant rice
1 cup chicken, cooked, diced
1 cup celery, chopped
2 tablespoons onion, chopped
1 teaspoon curry powder
1 teaspoon salt
$1/_2$ teaspoon dry mustard
$1/_4$ teaspoon pepper
$1/_2$ cup crushed pineapple
$1/_2$ cup mayonnaise

Combine boiling water with dry soup mix and rice; simmer until water is absorbed. Fluff rice with fork and allow to cool. Blend remaining ingredients with rice mixture. Cover and chill thoroughly.

"A personal favorite that serves as a main or side dish."

Patricia Johnson   **Iron Horse Middle School, San Ramon, CA**

Herbed Chicken Salad

Serves 4 - 6

$1/_4$ cup lemon juice
$1/_4$ cup oil
2 teaspoons chicken flavored bouillon
1 tablespoon sugar
1 teaspoon tarragon leaves
1 clove garlic, minced
3 cups chicken, cooked, cubed
1 cup mushrooms, sliced
$1/_2$ pound fresh green beans, cut into 1" pieces, cooked tender-crisp
1 cup cherry tomatoes, halved

In a small bowl, combine lemon juice, oil, bouillon, sugar, tarragon and garlic. Let stand 15 minutes to dissolve bouillon, stirring occasionally. In a large bowl, combine cooked chicken and mushrooms; pour dressing over and toss gently. Cover and chill 4 hours or overnight, stirring occasionally. Just before serving, stir in green beans and tomatoes.

"A friend brought this dish to a tailgate party.
It travels well and is light and refreshing on a hot day."

Cindy Peters   **Black Diamond Middle School, Antioch, CA**

NOTES & REMINDERS

Taco Salad

Serves 8

>   1 pound ground meat
>   1 package taco seasoning
>   2 heads lettuce, chopped
>   1 red onion, minced
>   1 can corn, drained
>   2 cans kidney, pinto or black beans, drained
>   1 carton refrigerated salsa
>   1 bunch cilantro, chopped
>   2 (small) cans black olives, sliced
>   2 cups sharp cheddar cheese, shredded
>   1 bag Fritos Chili Corn Chips
>   *Salad dressing:*
> $^1/_4$ cup lime juice
>   3 cloves garlic, minced
>   1 teaspoon cumin powder
>   3 packets Taco Bell hot sauce
> $^3/_4$ cup olive oil
>   salt, to taste

Brown ground meat with taco seasoning; drain. Toss with remaining lettuce, onion, corn, beans, salsa, cilantro, olives and cheese; chill. In a blender, make dressing by blending lime juice with garlic, cumin and hot sauce. Add olive oil in slow, steady stream. Salt to taste. To serve salad, add chips and dressing to chilled salad mixture and toss again.

"This salad pleases eaters of all ages!"

Vanessa Van Assen   **Fort Bragg High School, Fort Bragg, CA**

Tortellini Salad Toss

Serves 4

>   1 pound cheese tortellini
> $^1/_2$ cup sun-dried tomatoes
>   1 $^1/_2$ cups feta cheese, crumbled
> $^1/_2$ cup black olives, halved
> $^1/_2$ cup yellow bell pepper, chopped
>   2 tablespoons fresh basil, chopped
> $^1/_4$ cup red wine vinegar
> $^1/_4$ cup olive oil
>   salt, pepper, to taste

Cook and drain tortellini according to package directions. Cut sun-dried tomatoes into julienne strips. Add remaining ingredients and toss.

"Delicious as a hot or cold pasta salad."

Anne Silveira   **Shasta High School, Redding, CA**

NOTES & REMINDERS

34

World's Best Crab Pasta Salad

Serves 4 - 6

    1 package spiral noodles
    1 pound imitation crab meat, cubed
    1 cucumber, chopped
    1 bunch cilantro, chopped
    1 bunch green onion, chopped
    1 bottle Kraft ranch dressing

Cook noodles according to package directions; drain. Combine all ingredients and chill at least 4 hours before serving.

"This recipe was given to me by my friend, Rachel Rosen.
Salad is easy to make and quick to disappear. Yum!"

Cari Sheridan   **Grace Yokley School, Ontario, CA**

Summer Mac Salad

Serves 4 - 6

    8 ounces macaroni, cooked, drained
    1 cup onion, chopped
    1 cup celery, chopped
    $\frac{1}{2}$ cup carrot, shredded
    1 cup cucumber, chopped
    1 bunch broccoli florets
    $\frac{1}{2}$ cup mayonnaise
    $\frac{1}{2}$ cup oil
    $\frac{1}{4}$ cup vinegar
    $\frac{1}{4}$ cup sugar
    1 envelope Italian dressing mix

Combine macaroni, onion, celery, carrot, cucumber and broccoli in large bowl. In separate bowl, combine mayonnaise with oil, vinegar, sugar and Italian dressing mix. Toss with macaroni and chill until ready to serve.

"This recipe was given to me by my friend, Kitty Brown.
We served it for our 4th of July barbecue."

Deborah Weiss   **Ayala High School, Chino Hills, CA**

NOTES & REMINDERS

Greek Pasta Salad

Serves 8 - 10

>   1 (10 ounce) bag rainbow rotini pasta
>   2 cups cucumber, thinly sliced
>   1 (medium) tomato, chopped
>   1 (15 ounce) can garbanzo beans, drained
>   1 (2.25 ounce) can olives, sliced, drained
>   4 ounces basil & tomato flavored feta cheese, crumbled
> $1/4$ cup extra virgin olive oil
> $1/4$ cup lemon juice
> $1/4$ teaspoon salt
> $1/4$ cup parsley, finely chopped
>   Parmesan cheese, grated, to taste

Prepare pasta according to package directions; drain and rinse in cool water. Place in large bowl and add cucumber, tomato, beans, olives and cheese. In a jar with tight fitting lid, combine the remaining ingredients, except Parmesan cheese, and shake well. Toss with pasta and vegetables. Refrigerate 1 hour to blend flavors. Top with Parmesan cheese before serving.

"Use Roma tomatoes. Tastes better if refrigerated overnight. Adding cooked chicken makes a cool main dish for summer. Leave out the mayonnaise for a taste variation."

Suzi Schneider   **Bret Harte High School, Altaville, CA**
Kristine Carlin   **San Luis Obispo High School, SLO, CA**

Garden Gazpacho Pasta Salad

Serves 8

>   1 $1/2$ cups rotini pasta (4.5 ounces)
>   1 $1/2$ cups cheddar cheese, shredded
> $1/2$ cup olives, sliced
>   1 $1/2$ cups salsa
>   2 tablespoons vegetable oil
>   2 (small) zucchini, sliced
>   1 (large) tomato, chopped (1 cup)
>   1 (11 ounce) can whole kernel corn, drained

Cook and drain pasta as directed on package; rinse with cold water and drain. Toss pasta with remaining ingredients in large bowl. Serve immediately or cover and refrigerate up to 24 hours. Toss before serving.

"I like to refrigerate this before serving."

Christine Hindoian   **Granger High School, West Valley City, UT**

Santa Fe Chicken Pasta Salad

Serves 8

1 (16 ounce) package rotini pasta
Dressing:
1 $1/4$ cups V-8 juice
1 $1/2$ tablespoons olive oil
1 tablespoon red wine vinegar
1 $1/2$ teaspoons chili powder
$3/4$ teaspoon paprika
$1/2$ teaspoon salt
$1/4$ teaspoon black pepper
$1/2$ cup Parmesan cheese, grated
$1/2$ cup yellow corn kernels, cooked
$1/3$ cup cilantro, chopped
$1/4$ cup green onion, chopped
2 tablespoons red bell pepper, diced
2 tablespoons green pepper, diced
1 boneless chicken breast, cooked, diced

Prepare pasta according to package directions. Whisk all dressing ingredients together. Cover and chill until ready to use. Combine cooked pasta with dressing and remaining ingredients. Chill several hours.

Jill Burnham   **Bloomington High School, Bloomington, CA**

Easy Rainbow Pasta Salad

Serves 12

1 box rainbow corkscrew pasta
1 can whole (medium or large) olives
10 cherry tomatoes, cut in half OR 20 mini-pear shaped tomatoes
1 red bell pepper, cut into 1" squares
1 orange or yellow bell pepper, cut into 1" squares
1 (large) can artichoke hearts in water, cut in half or quarters
1 carrot, peeled, sliced diagonally $1/4$" wide, blanched
1 celery stick, sliced diagonally $1/4$" wide
1 bottle Robust or Creamy Italian salad dressing

Cook pasta according to package directions; rinse and drain. Place in a large serving bowl. Add prepared vegetables, pour half of the dressing over pasta and toss. Chill and serve, adding more dressing to taste, if needed. NOTE: To blanch vegetables, immerse in boiling water for 2 to 3 minutes, then remove and immerse in ice water to bring out color and soften texture slightly. VARIATIONS: You can also use green peppers, green onions, and/or blanched broccoli.

Debbie Warren   **Hueneme High School, Oxnard, CA**

NOTES & REMINDERS

Chop Stick Salad

Serves 6 - 8

> 1 package Chicken Rice-A-Roni
> 1 cup green onions, sliced
> 1 can water sliced chestnuts, drained
> 1 (small) jar pimientos, diced
> 1 jar marinated artichoke hearts, with liquid
> $1/4$ cup mayonnaise

Cook rice according to package directions, using $1/4$ cup less water. Fluff with fork the last few minutes of cooking; let cool. Add remaining ingredients being sure to include liquid from artichoke hearts; mix well. Chill 2 to 3 hours before serving. NOTE: Recipe is easily doubled.

"Great salad to take to a party or barbecue. Can be made the night before. Because of the green onions and red pimiento, it looks festive for Christmas too!"

Carolyn Helmle   **Tokay High School, Lodi, CA**

Rice-Artichoke Salad

Serves 4 - 6

> 1 package MJB Chicken Flavored Rice
> 4 green onions, chopped
> $3/4$ cup celery, chopped
> $1/2$ cup green pepper, chopped
> 12 green olives, sliced
> 2 jars marinated artichoke hearts, drained, reserve liquid
> $1/3$ cup mayonnaise
> $1/2$ teaspoon curry powder

Cook rice according to package directions, leaving out butter; cool. Stir in onion, celery, green pepper and olives. Drain liquid from artichokes, reserving liquid. Add artichokes to rice. In small bowl, combine liquid from artichokes with mayonnaise and curry powder. Toss dressing with rice mixture; chill before serving.

"Delicious served with barbecued foods."

Joan Wayland   **O.W. Holmes Junior High School, Davis, CA**

NOTES & REMINDERS

Real Old Fashioned Potato Salad

Serves 8 - 10

 5 pounds potatoes, cooked, diced
 6 green onions OR $^1/_2$ cup red onion, chopped
 6 eggs, boiled, peeled, chopped
 $^1/_2$ cup dill pickles, chopped
 $^1/_2$ cup sweet pickles, chopped
 1 cup olives, chopped
 2 cups Best Foods mayonnaise
 2 tablespoons prepared mustard
 1 teaspoon salt
 1 teaspoon pepper
 1 teaspoon Morton's seasoning salt
 $^1/_4$ cup sweet pickle juice
 dash paprika

Mix first 6 ingredients together in large bowl. Reserve 1 egg for garnish. In separate bowl, stir together mayonnaise, mustard, spices and pickle juice. Pour over potato mixture and toss to coat. Garnish with sliced egg and sprinkle with paprika. Chill.

"I always get wonderful comments on this recipe.
It even tastes good before being chilled!"

Elizabeth Thornburg   **Selma High School, Selma, CA**

My Mom's Potato Salad

Serves 6 - 8

 5 to 6 (medium) potatoes
 1 cup Best Food's mayonnaise
 2 tablespoons Heinz yellow mustard
 1 teaspoon horseradish
 $^3/_4$ of a (7 ounce) jar stuffed green olives, sliced
 1 (medium) onion, finely chopped
 salt, to taste

Cook potatoes, with jackets on, in lightly salted water until tender; drain and cool. Remove skins and cut into cubes. Using a whisk, beat together the mayonnaise, mustard and horseradish. Fold dressing into potatoes. Add sliced olives and onions. Salt to taste. Refrigerate. NOTE: This is best if made a day ahead.

"Making potato salad is not an exact science. When I asked my mother for her recipe, it
started as a little of this and a little of that! We have done our best."

Gayle Grigg   **Hendrix Junior High School, Chandler, AZ**

NOTES & REMINDERS

39

Lowfat Potato Salad

Serves 10

> 2 cloves garlic, peeled, halved
> 3 tablespoons olive oil
> I cup tarragon wine vinegar
> I teaspoon salt
> I teaspoon sugar
> I tablespoon fresh dill
> 4 eggs, hard cooked, peeled, chopped
> 3 pounds white rose or red potatoes (about 6 large)
> 3 green onions, sliced
> $^1/_2$ cup red onion, diced
> I cup celery, chopped (2 or 3 stalks)
> $^1/_2$ cup red bell pepper, diced
> $^1/_2$ cup mayonnaise
> $^1/_2$ cup nonfat sour cream

To make dressing, combine garlic and oil in small bowl. Let stand at least 10 minutes; discard garlic. Stir in vinegar, salt, sugar and dill weed; set aside. Prepare eggs and chill until needed. Scrub potatoes and cook in boiling water until tender through when pierced with fork, about 20 to 30 minutes. Drain and let cool briefly, leaving skins on; cut into $^1/_2$" cubes. Place in large salad bowl and add dressing, gently tossing to coat. Cover and refrigerate at least 1 hour (or until next day). After potatoes have absorbed dressing, add onions, celery and bell pepper. Chop eggs and sprinkle over potatoes. Add mayonnaise and sour cream; spoon over potato mixture, stirring gently to coat potatoes evenly. Cover and chill 4 to 6 hours.

"Even my husband, who normally hates 'low fat' versions, likes this potato salad!"
Ellen Gordon   **Colton High School, Colton, CA**

Calico Dilly Potato Salad

Serves 8

> I $^1/_2$ pounds (small) new red potatoes
> $^1/_4$ teaspoon salt
> $^1/_4$ cup olive oil
> 2 tablespoons white wine vinegar
> I tablespoon fresh dill weed
> I tablespoon prepared mustard
> $^1/_2$ teaspoon sugar
> $^1/_4$ teaspoon seasoned salt
> dash white pepper
> $^3/_4$ cup red bell pepper
> $^3/_4$ cup green pepper
> $^1/_2$ cup red onion, diced
> I cup frozen peas, thawed
> $^1/_4$ cup green onion, sliced

Place potatoes and salt in medium saucepan. Add enough water to cover and bring to a boil. Cook over medium heat 15 to 20 minutes, or until potatoes are tender; drain. Let cool slightly, then quarter potatoes. In a jar with a lid, combine olive oil, wine vinegar, dill weed, mustard, sugar, salt and pepper; shake well and pour over potatoes. Combine with bell peppers, red onion, peas and green onions. Cover and refrigerate several hours to blend flavors.

Doreen Lee   **Ralph Waldo Emerson Junior High School, Davis, CA**

Strawberry Jell-O Salad

Serves 8 - 12

    2 (6 ounce) packages strawberry jello
    1 $1/2$ cups boiling water
    1 (20 ounce) can crushed pineapple, with juice
    1 $1/2$ cups cold water
    1 (8 ounce) package cream cheese, softened
    1 (8 ounce) package cottage cheese
    1 (16 ounce) bag frozen strawberries, sliced
    1 $1/2$ cups heavy whipping cream, whipped
    1 cup walnuts, chopped (optional)

Dissolve jello in boiling water in large mixing bowl. Add crushed pineapple with juice and cold water. Refrigerate until mostly congealed. Beat in cream cheese and cottage cheese with electric mixer. Fold in cut strawberries and whipped cream. Fold in chopped nuts, if using. Refrigerate to set.

"A delightful salad with a heavy meal."

Becky Oppen   **Dana Hills High School, Dana Point, CA**

Strawberry Pretzel Jell-O

Serves 10 - 12

    2 $1/2$ cups pretzels, crushed
    $3/4$ cup butter, melted
    1 cup + 3 tablespoons sugar, divided
    1 (8 ounce) package cream cheese, softened
    1 (10 ounce) container whipped topping
    1 (6 ounce) package strawberry jello
    2 cups boiling water
    2 (10 ounce) packages frozen strawberries, with juice, thawed

Combine pretzels, butter and 3 tablespoons sugar; spread into a 9" x 13" pan. Bake at 350 degrees for 10 minutes. Cool completely. Mix together cream cheese, 1 cup sugar and whipped topping; spread over pretzel crust. Dissolve jello in water; add strawberries and chill until partially thickened. Spoon on to cream cheese. Chill until firm.

Joan Tucker   **Vacaville High School, Vacaville, CA**

Grandma Hampton's Strawberry Salad

Serves 8

> 3 bananas
> 1 can crushed pineapple, drained
> 2 packages sweetened strawberries, thawed
> 1 (6 ounce) package strawberry/banana jello
> 1 cup boiling water
> 1 pint sour cream

Mash bananas; add drained pineapple. Stir in thawed strawberries, including juice; set aside. Stir jello into boiling water. Add to strawberries and mix well. Pour half into a 9" x 13" glass dish and chill until firm, 2 to 3 hours. Spread sour cream on top. Add last layer using remaining mixture. Chill.

"A family favorite from Mildred Evelyn Hampton, passed down two generations."
Melissa Webb   **Lakewood High School, Lakewood, CA**

Rainbow Ribbon Jell-O Salad

Serves 6

> 5 (3 ounce) packages jello (assorted flavors/colors)
> 7 1/2 cups boiling water, divided
> 1 cup sour cream

Dissolve one package jello in 1 1/2 cups boiling water. Pour 3/4 cup mixture into a 6 cup ring mold or a 9" square pan. Chill until set, but not firm, about 15 minutes. With remaining gelatin, mix in 3 tablespoons sour cream; pour over clear layer when set. Repeat with each remaining flavor of jello. Be sure to chill before pouring onto set layers. Chill at least 2 hours.

"This looks great when unmolded and kids love it!"
Pamela Campion   **Dublin High School, Dublin , CA**

Orva's Special Lime Salad

Serves 8

> 1 package lemon jello
> 1 package lime jello
> 2 cups hot water
> 1 (14 ounce) can crushed pineapple
> 1 cup Cool Whip
> 1 (16 ounce) container cottage cheese
> 1 cup mayonnaise
> 1/2 cup nuts
> 2 tablespoons horseradish

Dissolve jellos in hot water; cool. Add pineapple with juice and allow to thicken. Stir in remaining ingredients and pour into a 13" x 9" glass pan. Refrigerate overnight.

Sonja Tyree   **Ayala High School, Chino Hills, CA**

Cherry Coke Jell-O Salad
Serves 8

    1 (#2) can dark bing cherries, cut in half
    1 (#2) can crushed pineapple
    2 (small) packages cherry jello
    1 (12 ounce) can cola

Drain juices from fruit; set fruit aside. Place juice in saucepan and heat to simmer. Dissolve jello in juice, mixing well. Add cola and fruit, stirring well. Place in refrigerator until firm.

Debbie L. Rothe   **Alta Loma High School, Alta Loma, CA**

Bing Cherry Cola Salad
Serves 6

    1 (1 pound) can bing cherries
    1 (4 ounce) can pineapple chunks
    1 (large) package black cherry jello
    1 (12 ounce) can cola
    1 (8 ounce) package cream cheese
    1 container Cool Whip

Drain cherries and pineapple. Combine juices to make 2 $\frac{1}{2}$ cups liquid (add water if necessary). Heat juices and pour over gelatin, stirring until dissolved. Add cherries, pineapple and cola. Chill until it begins to thicken. Cut cream cheese into small cubes and stir into partially thickened gelatin. Pour into a 1 $\frac{1}{4}$ quart ring mold or 9" x 13" oblong dish. Chill until firm. Frost with Cool Whip.

"This is a family recipe from 30 years ago."

Pam Fecchino   **Cimarron-Memorial High School, Las Vegas, NV**

Pastel Jell-O Salad
Serves 15

    1 (large) can pears
    1 (large) package lime jello
    1 (8 ounce) package cream cheese
    1 (8 ounce) Cool Whip

Drain pears and dissolve lime jello in juice. In blender, blend pears with cream cheese. Add pear juice and jello and continue to blend until all ingredients are mixed together. Blend in Cool Whip. Pour into glass 9" x 13" pan. Chill.

"Economical and very good! Utah is the Jell-O Capital of the world, after all!"

Pasty Graves   **Bingham High School, So. Jordan, UT**

Frozen Fruit Salad

Serves 10

> 1 (11 ounce) can mandarin orange sections
> 1 (3 ounce) package lime gelatin
> 1 cup boiling water
> 1 cup sour cream
> $1/2$ cup mayonnaise
> 1 cup miniature marshmallows
> $1/4$ cup nuts, chopped

Drain orange sections, reserving syrup. Add water to syrup to make $1/2$ cup; set aside. Dissolve gelatin in boiling water. Add reserved syrup and chill until slightly thickened. Blend sour cream and mayonnaise into gelatin; chill again until thickened. Fold in orange sections, marshmallows and nuts. Spoon into 8" square pan or 8" x 4" loaf pan and freeze until firm. Unmold and garnish with crisp salad greens and additional fruit, if desired.

"Can be made ahead of time and makes a nice contrast with barbecued meats."
Pam Bonilla   **Valley View High School, Moreno Valley, CA**

Lemon Fruit Salad

Serves 20 - 24

> 2 (11 ounce) cans mandarin orange sections
> 2 (8.75 ounce) cans peaches, diced
> 2 (8.75 ounce) cans pineapple tidbits
> 1 (15 ounce) can fruit cocktail
> 1 (3.25 ounce) package instant lemon pudding mix
> 1 (3.25 ounce) package tapioca pudding mix
> 4 tablespoons lemon juice
> 2 cups miniature marshmallows
> 4 cups frozen whipped topping, thawed

Drain fruits; reserve 3 cups syrup. Prepare pudding according to package directions, substituting reserved 3 cups syrup for milk called for on package. Prepare tapioca according to package directions; stir in lemon juice; cool. Combine both puddings. Fold drained fruit and marshmallows into puddings. Fold in whipped topping. Chill well, preferably overnight.

"This is an easy make ahead dish."
Astrid Curfman   **Newcomb Academy, Long Beach, CA**

NOTES & REMINDERS

Cookie Fruit Salad

Serves 10

> 1 (large) package instant vanilla pudding mix
> 1 $^1/_2$ cups milk
> 16 ounces Cool Whip
> 2 (11 ounce) cans mandarin oranges, drained
> 1 (20 ounce) can chunk pineapple, drained
> 1 package Mother's striped chocolate shortbread cookies, crushed
> 1 to 2 bananas, sliced

Mix pudding and milk together with a wire whisk. Add Cool Whip and mix well. Fold in remaining ingredients and chill before serving.

Maria Montemagni   **Mt. Whitney High School, Visalia, CA**

Fast Fruit Salad

Serves 4

> 4 ounces cream cheese, at room temperature
> 2 tablespoons lemon juice
> 1 Fuji apple, cored, cut into bite-sized pieces
> 1 cup seedless red grapes
> 1 (11 ounce) can mandarin oranges, drained, cut in half
> 1 (5.5 ounce) can pineapple chunks, drained

With an electric mixer, whip cream cheese with lemon juice until fluffy. Add remaining ingredients; fold together and serve chilled.

Julie Eyre   **Alhambra High School, Alhambra, CA**

Baked Garlic and Onion Cream Soup

Serves 6 - 8

> 6 (large) onions, sliced into $^1/_2$" slices
> 2 heads garlic, cloves separated and peeled
> 5 cups chicken broth, divided
> 1 $^1/_2$ teaspoon dried thyme leaves
> 1 teaspoon kosher salt
> 1 teaspoon coarsely ground black pepper
> 4 tablespoons unsalted butter
> 2 cups heavy whipping cream
> 2 tablespoons Italian parsley, chopped

Preheat oven to 350 degrees. Place onions and garlic into shallow roasting pan. Add 3 cups chicken broth, thyme, salt and pepper. Dot with butter. Cover with foil and bake 1 $^1/_2$ hours. Stir once or twice while baking. Remove from oven and puree in food processor until smooth. With motor running, gradually add remaining 2 cups chicken broth and cream. Pour soup into large saucepan and adjust seasonings. Heat slowly and thoroughly. Sprinkle with parsley and serve.

Stephanie San Sebastian   **Central High School, Fresno, CA**

NOTES & REMINDERS

Taco Soup
Serves 8 - 10

I pound ground beef or turkey
I onion
I can kidney
I can pinto beans
I can black beans
I can chopped tomatoes
I can corn
I small jar mild salsa
I teaspoon taco seasoning
Garnishes: Shredded cheese, sliced olives, sour cream, cilantro
corn chips

Brown ground beef or turkey with onion; drain fat. Add beans, tomatoes and corn, including liquid. Stir in salsa and taco seasoning. Let simmer until flavors blend, at least 1 hour. Top with desired garnishes and serve, with corn chips. NOTE: This may be made in a crock pot and cooked on low all day. It also freezes well.

Lura Staffanson   **Centennial High School, Corona, CA**

Side Dishes

Baked Beans & Ham Hocks

Serves 8 - 10

> 1 package small white beans
> 1 (large) can tomatoes
> 1 (large) onion, chopped
> $^1/_2$ pound brown sugar
> 2 to 3 ham hocks

Soak white beans in water overnight. Then, parboil for 20 minutes, pouring off liquid. Add remaining ingredients. Bake in a covered casserole dish at 300 degrees for 6 hours, adding more liquid, if desired.

"Delicious. Nice for a large group."

Laurie Hollman   **Porterville High School, Porterville, CA**

Shirley Beans

Makes 4 quarts

> 1 pound ground beef
> 1 onion, chopped
> 1 pound bacon
> 2 (29 ounce) cans pork 'n beans
> 1 (16 ounce) can kidney beans
> 1 (16 ounce) can lima beans
> 1 (16 ounce) can butter beans
> 1 cup catsup
> $^1/_2$ to 1 cup dark brown sugar
> 1 tablespoon white vinegar
> 2 tablespoons liquid smoke

Cook ground beef and onion together; drain excess fat. Cook bacon; drain and crumble. Drain some of the liquid off pork 'n beans and most of the liquid from other beans. Combine all ingredients in crock pot and cook, covered for 4 to 6 hours.

"The liquid smoke adds a wonderful flavor. My nieces call these Shirley Beans. You can leave out the bacon and beef and these still taste great!"

Shirley Marshman   **West Middle School, Downey, CA**

NOTES & REMINDERS

47

Sweet & Sour Baked Beans

Serves 8 -10

    1 (28 ounce) can pork 'n beans
    $^1/_2$ pound bacon
    $^1/_4$ (medium) onion, diced
    1 (medium) green pepper, chopped
    1 tablespoon Worcestershire sauce
    $^3/_4$ cup catsup
    $^1/_2$ cup brown sugar
    1 (8 ounce) can pineapple tidbits, with juice
    2 tablespoons corn starch (optional)
    $^1/_2$ cup cold water (optional)

Pour pork 'n beans into crock pot. Chop bacon into $^1/_4$" pieces and brown slightly, for 2 to 3 minutes. Add to beans. Stir in onion, green pepper, Worcestershire sauce, catsup, brown sugar and pineapple, with juice. Cook on HIGH for 8 hours. If desired, thicken with cornstarch mixed in cold water.

"In a large 3 to 4 quart crockpot, double the recipe. It will feed a crowd of 20+!"
LeeAnn Bitner   **Alta High School, Sandy, UT**

Calico Beans

Serves 16

    3 strips bacon
    1 onion, chopped
    1 (16 ounce) can kidney beans, drained
    1 (16 ounce) can lima beans, drained
    1 (16 ounce) can butter beans, drained
    1 (16 ounce) can pork 'n beans
    $^3/_4$ cup catsup
    $^3/_4$ cup brown sugar
    1 tablespoon Worcestershire sauce
    1 cup cheddar cheese, shredded

Cook bacon until crisp; remove from pan and crumble; set aside. Sauté onion in bacon grease. Combine everything in a casserole dish. Sprinkle bacon on top. Cook, covered, for 1 hour at 350 degrees.

"This recipe is a delightful change for baked beans, given to me by a special friend."
Amy Tavaglione-Rudolph   **Etiwanda High School, Etiwanda, CA**

Betty's Corn Pudding

Serves 4 - 6

  1 (14 ounce) can creamed corn
  1 (14 ounce) can whole kernel corn, drained
  1 box Jiffy corn muffin mix
  1 cube butter, melted
  1 cup sour cream
  2 eggs

Mix all ingredients in casserole dish and bake at 350 degrees for 1 hour.

"This is Betty Jo Bethke's recipe. When she brings it to a pot luck,
she always leaves with an empty dish!"

Donna Long   **South Hills High School, West Covina, CA**

Bertie's Baked Shoestring Potatoes

Serves 4

  Aluminum foil
  4 (medium) potatoes
  3 tablespoons butter or margarine
  1 $1/2$ teaspoons salt
  dash pepper
  $1/2$ cup sharp processed American cheese, grated
  2 tablespoons parsley, chopped
  $1/2$ cup light or heavy cream

Cut a 48" length of aluminum foil and fold in half. Cut potatoes like French fries and place just off center on foil. Dot with butter. Sprinkle with salt, pepper, cheese and parsley. Pull edges of foil upward, then pour cream over potatoes. Fold to seal. Cook over glowing coals on the barbecue or in a 450 degree oven for about 1 hour or until done. Serve from package.

"Bertie Kamps, my mom, used to make these potatoes
when we would barbecue with my Aunt Ann's family. They are still great!"

Barbara Schollenberg   **Grace Davis High School, Modesto, CA**

Funeral Potatoes

Serves 10

  $1/2$ cup butter or margarine
  1 (1 pound) package frozen cubed hash browned potatoes
  $1/2$ cup minced onion
  2 cups cheddar cheese, shredded
  2 cups sour cream
  1 can cream of mushroom soup
  $1/2$ cup crumbs (bread or corn flakes)

Preheat oven to 350 degrees. Melt margarine or butter. In a bowl, combine all ingredients, except crumbs. Spread mixture evenly in a greased 9" x 13" baking pan.

Sprinkle crumbs on top, cover with foil and bake at 350 degrees for 1 hour. Remove foil last 15 minutes. NOTE: Dehydrated onions can be substituted for fresh. Cream of chicken soup may be substituted for cream of mushroom. This can be made ahead and baked later.

"My sister shared this. Everyone in her town (population 75) takes these to the potlucks after funerals. Her preschool students named them funeral potatoes.*"*

April Rosendahl   **Chino High School, Chino, CA**

Party Potatoes

Serves 8 - 10

> 4 pounds potatoes, peeled
> 1 (8 ounce) package cream cheese
> $1/2$ cup sour cream
> $1/3$ cup butter
> 1 teaspoon salt
> $1/8$ teaspoon pepper
> paprika

Boil potatoes until tender; drain. Beat with electric beater. Add next five ingredients and beat until fluffy. Spoon into a buttered baking dish. Garnish with paprika. Bake at 350 degrees for 30 minutes.

"Great for a party because this dish can be made up in advance and then heated."

Susan Lefler   **Ramona Junior High School, Chino, CA**

Potatoes Royale

Serves 8 - 10

> 8 slices bacon
> 8 (medium) potatoes, peeled
> $1/2$ cup onion, chopped
> $1/2$ cup water
> 1 cup mayonnaise
> $2/3$ cup sour cream
> 2 cups cheddar cheese, shredded
> $1/2$ cup stuffed green olives, sliced
> 1 teaspoon salt
> $1/8$ teaspoon pepper

Place bacon between layers of paper toweling on a glass plate. Microwave on HIGH 6 to 7 minutes or until crisp; set aside. Slice potatoes into a 2 quart casserole dish; add onion and water. Cover with lid or plastic wrap and microwave on HIGH until potatoes are tender, approximately 26 minutes, stirring every 6 minutes; drain. Combine remaining ingredients; mix lightly to combine. Crumble bacon and sprinkle over top. Microwave on HIGH, uncovered, 3 to 4 minutes or until heated through.

Rhonda Nelson   **Rancho Santa Margarita Intermediate, RSM, CA**

Ranch Mashed Potatoes

Serves 4

> 6 (large) potatoes
> $1/4$ to $1/2$ cup ranch style dressing
> salt and pepper
> 1 $1/2$ to 2 cups mozzarella cheese, shredded
> 3 tablespoons butter
> $1/2$ to 1 cup milk

Peel, cube and boil potatoes until tender; drain water. Add ranch dressing, salt and pepper, grated mozzarella and butter. Mix with electric mixer, adding milk, until desired consistency is achieved.

"You can substitute different kinds of cheese."

Rhonda Pratt   **Joe Walker Junior High School, Quartz Hill, CA**

Scalloped Potatoes

Serves 10 - 12

> 12 potatoes
> 2 cans cheddar cheese soup
> 2 cans milk
> $1/4$ to $1/2$ teaspoon pepper
> $1/2$ teaspoon salt
> $1/2$ to 1 cup onions, chopped or sliced
> $1/2$ cup Parmesan cheese, grated

Wash potatoes, peel thinly and remove eyes. Cut into thin slices, making about 8 cups. Mix cheddar cheese soup, milk and spices together. In greased 9" x 13" casserole, arrange potatoes in 2 layers, topping each layer with half the onions and half the grated cheese and half the soup mixture. Repeat layers and bake at 350 degrees for 1 hour.

Darlene Lupul   **Tokay High School, Lodi, CA**

Tater Tot Casserole

Serves 8 - 10

2 teaspoons butter or nonstick cooking spray
2 eggs
2 cups milk
salt and pepper, to taste
2 cups yellow cheddar cheese, grated, divided
2 cups white cheddar cheese, grated, divided
1 (2 pound) bag tater tots, thawed
1 cup ham, diced (optional)
1/2 cup green peppers, chopped (optional)
1/2 cup onion, chopped (optional)
Variation:
1 (2 pound) bag tater tots, thawed
1 can cream of chicken soup
1 1/2 cups light sour cream
3 cups cheese, shredded
salt and pepper, to taste
1 cup corn flakes, crushed

Grease a 9" x 13" baking pan with butter or nonstick cooking spray. In a very large mixing bowl, whisk eggs, milk, salt and pepper. Add 1 cup yellow and 1 cup white cheddar cheese. Stir in tater tots and optional items, if desired. Mix thoroughly and pour into prepared pan. Sprinkle with remaining cheeses. Bake at 350 degrees until top is golden brown, 45 to 60 minutes. Variation: Spread tater tots in pan. In a bowl, mix soup with sour cream and half of the cheese. Spread mixture over tater tots. Sprinkle with remaining cheese and crushed corn flakes. Bake 1 hour at 350 degrees.

"An easy side dish that can be made ahead and baked while meat is grilling!"
Ruth Anne Mills   **Los Alisos Intermediate School, Mission Viejo, CA**

Slow Roasted Tomatoes

Serves 8

4 pounds plum tomatoes
6 cloves garlic, minced
5 tablespoons olive oil
salt
ground pepper

Heat oven to 200 degrees. Wash tomatoes and cut in half lengthwise. Place on shallow baking sheet, cut side up. Combine garlic and oil, then spoon over tomatoes. Season with salt and pepper. Place pan in oven to roast 6 to 8 hours, turning 2 to 3 times during cooking.

"Store in an airtight container, chilled. They can be used in salads, pastas, or on toasted bread. Warm to room temperature before using."
Sue Ballard   **Silverado High School, Victorville, CA**

Rancho California Rice

Serves 8 - 10

- 1 cup onion, chopped
- 4 tablespoons butter
- 4 cups rice, cooked
- 2 cups sour cream
- 1 cup cottage cheese
- 1 bay leaf, crumbled
- salt and pepper, to taste
- 2 (4 ounce) cans diced green chiles
- 2 cups extra sharp cheddar cheese, grated (reserve $1/3$ cup for topping)

In a large skillet, sauté onions in butter until limp. Add rice, sour cream, cottage cheese, bay leaf, and salt and pepper, to taste. In a greased casserole, put a layer of rice; then chiles and cheese. Repeat, ending with layer of rice. Bake 25 minutes at 375 degrees. Remove from oven and sprinkle with $1/3$ cup reserved grated cheese. Bake 10 minutes more.

Sheri Rader   **Chaparral High School, Las Vegas, NV**

Connie's Broccoli Rice

Serves 8 - 10

- 1 (medium) onion, chopped
- $3/4$ cube butter
- 1 (large) bag broccoli, thawed and drained
- 2 cups white rice, cooked
- 1 (8 ounce) jar Cheez Whiz
- 1 can cream of mushroom soup
- 1 cup cheddar cheese, grated

Preheat oven to 350 degrees. Sauté onion in butter; set aside. Combine broccoli, rice, Cheez Whiz and soup; mix well. Add sautéed onion and turn into a greased 9" x 12" baking dish. Sprinkle with grated cheese. Bake for 30 minutes.

"This is a family favorite prepared by my sister-in-law, Connie Henderson, for all occasions."

Gerry Henderson   **Temple City High School, Temple City, CA**

Broccoli Casserole

Serves 8 - 12

- 2 (10 ounce) packages frozen chopped broccoli
- $1/2$ cup mayonnaise
- 1 can cream of mushroom soup
- 1 (medium) onion, finely chopped
- 2 cups sharp cheddar cheese, grated
- 2 eggs
- 1 cup Ritz crackers, chopped

Cook frozen broccoli as directed on package. Drain and mix with remaining ingredients, except crackers. Place in an 8" x 8" baking dish and add crushed crackers on top. Bake at 350 degrees for 30 minutes.

"This is a big favorite at my exercise class potlucks."

Ruth Anne Schroeder   **River City HS, West Sacramento, CA**

Zucchini Casserole with Crumb Topping

Serves 4 - 6

1 onion, finely chopped
2 tablespoons butter
3 cups zucchini, grated
3 eggs, beaten
$1/2$ cup sour cream
$1/2$ cup pancake flour
salt and pepper, to taste
$1/4$ cup Ritz cracker crumbs
$1/4$ cup Parmesan cheese, grated

Sauté onion in butter until soft. Add zucchini and sauté until almost tender. Place mixture in a greased 9" baking pan or dish. Beat together eggs, sour cream, flour, salt and pepper until blended. Pour mixture over zucchini. Sprinkle top with cracker crumbs and grated Parmesan. Bake at 350 degrees for about 30 minutes, or until casserole is golden and puffy.

Roberta Marshall   **Deer Valley High School, Antioch, CA**

Veggie Crisp

Serves 6 - 8

1 can French cut green beans
1 (small) can peas
4 stalks celery, chopped
$1/4$ cup onion, chopped
1 green pepper, chopped
1 (small) can pimiento, optional
1 teaspoon salt
$3/4$ cup sugar
$1/2$ cup vinegar
$1/4$ cup vegetable oil
1 tablespoon water

Drain green beans and peas. Place in 2 quart container with lid. Chop celery, onion and green pepper and add to beans. Stir in pimiento. In small bowl, mix together salt, sugar, vinegar, oil and water until sugar is dissolved. Pour over vegetables, cover with lid and let marinate overnight. Drain before serving, reserving liquid to store leftovers.

"Very colorful. It keeps a long time in the refrigerator."

Paula Schaefer   **Garside Junior High School, Las Vegas, NV**

NOTES & REMINDERS

Pineapple Casserole

Serves 6 - 8

$1/4$ cup butter
$3/4$ cup sugar
4 eggs
1 (20 ounce) can crushed pineapple, drained
5 slices bread, cubed

Cream butter and sugar; add eggs and mix. Stir in pineapple and bread cubes to coat. Pour into greased casserole. Bake 1 hour at 350 degrees.

"This is a delicious side dish for ham. Nyla Mahood's friends even eat it for dessert! Thanks, Nyla, an alumnus of Valley High School!"

Mary M. Rector   **Valley High School, Las Vegas, NV**

Marinated Grilled Vegetables

Serves 4 - 6

1 bulb garlic
$1/3$ cup + 2 teaspoons olive oil
1 (small) zucchini
1 yellow summer squash
8 ounces green beans
6 ounces baby carrots
1 (large) onion, cut into sections
1 (small) can whole potatoes, cut in half
8 ounces (small) fresh mushrooms
1 (small) can baby corn, drained
2 tablespoons seasoned rice vinegar
1 tablespoon basil or thyme (or combination), chopped
Grill basket

Preheat oven to 350 degrees. Cut the top off the garlic bulb, leaving it attached at the root. Drizzle a small amount (2 teaspoons) of olive oil over it. Wrap in aluminum foil and roast for 20 to 30 minutes in oven. Meanwhile, clean and cut all vegetables. Remove garlic and scrape into a large mixing bowl. Add $1/3$ cup olive oil and vinegar; whisk together. Add herbs and mix well. Toss with vegetables and allow to marinate at room temperature, tossing a few times to be sure all vegetables are coated with marinade. Heat grill to high heat. Place basket on grill to heat. Add vegetables and close the cover or cover with foil. Stir fry the vegetables, using a long handled spoon or pancake turner, every 3 minutes. Cook until desired doneness, about 10 minutes. Do not overcook.

"I bought my grill basket at Target. It looks like a square basket that has holes in it."

Sandy Hughes   **Upland High School, Upland, CA**

NOTES & REMINDERS

Grilled Fresh Vegetables

Serves 4

> 2 tablespoons butter
> 2 tablespoons olive oil
> 2 cloves garlic, minced
> 2 fresh summer squash, thinly sliced
> 1 zucchini, thinly sliced
> 1 portabello mushroom, thinly sliced
> salt and pepper, to taste

NOTES & REMINDERS

Melt butter in a small saucepan; add oil and heat until medium-hot. Add garlic and sauté 1 minute. Wash and slice squash and mushroom. Heat grill until hot. Brush vegetables with oil mixture, sprinkle with salt and pepper and place right on the hot grill. Grill for 5 minutes, turn and grill other side. Remove and serve.

"Great side dish for any grilled main course."

Jane Souza   **No. Monterey Co. High School, Castroville, CA**

Grilled Tomatoes

Serves 4

> 2 large tomatoes
> 2 tablespoons mayonnaise
> 2 tablespoons Parmesan cheese, grated, divided
> $1/4$ teaspoon basil
> $1/8$ teaspoon garlic or onion powder

Cut each tomato into 4 slices. Combine mayonnaise with 1 tablespoon Parmesan cheese, basil and garlic or onion powder. Mix well and spread slices with mixture. Sprinkle with additional 1 tablespoon Parmesan cheese. Broil until bubbly. Do not overcook - they will become mushy.

"If you love tomatoes, this is a delicious side dish for
any grilled meat and salad picnic supper!"

Carol Winter   **Hillcrest High School, Midvale, UT**

Grilled Vegetable Platter

Serves 6   *Photo opporite page 64*

> 1 cup Lawry's Mediterranean Marinade with Lemon Juice
> 12 (small) portabello mushrooms, cut into $1/2$" slices
> 2 zucchini or yellow squash, cut into $1/2$" slices
> 1 (small) onion, cut into wedges
> 1 (small) Japanese eggplant, cut into $1/2$" slices
> 2 red, green and/or yellow bell peppers, cut into chunks

In large Ziploc bag, combine all ingredients; mix well. Seal bag and marinate in refrigerator at least 30 minutes. Remove vegetables; reserve used marinade. Grill or broil mixed vegetables 10 to 12 minutes or until tender (mushrooms cook quickly), turning once and basting often with reserved marinade. Vegetables should be slightly "charred". Arrange vegetables on platter and serve. NOTE: If oven roasting, preheat oven to 450 degrees. Root vegetables should be covered and roasted 20 minutes. Uncover and continue roasting 20 to 25 minutes, or until tender. Non-root vegetables (peppers, mushrooms, squash, eggplant, etc.) should be roasted, uncovered, about 20 to 25 minutes or until tender. VARIATION: Place vegetables on skewers and grill over medium heat to desired doneness.

"Great picnic side dish, to top a main dish salad, to wrap in a tortilla or to add to a sandwich. Can be made ahead and kept in refrigerator until ready to use."

Lawry's Foods, Inc.   **Monrovia, CA**

Garlic Bread

Serves 8

$1/2$ pound margarine, softened
$1/2$ pound New York cheddar cheese, grated
$1/4$ cup Romano cheese, grated
$1/4$ teaspoon garlic powder
1 loaf French bread, sliced

Mix together margarine, cheeses and garlic powder. Spread on thick slices of French bread. Place under broiler and cook until cheese is melted. Serve immediately.

Jan Neufeld   **Fullerton High School, Fullerton, CA**

French Cheese Bread

Serves 8

1 cup Best Foods mayonnaise
$1/4$ pound sharp cheddar cheese, grated
$1/2$ (medium) onion, grated
1 teaspoon Worcestershire sauce
1 loaf sour French baguette, thinly sliced

In a small bowl, combine first 4 ingredients. Spread on baguette slices. Place on baking sheet. Broil until lightly browned and bubbly. Serve hot. NOTE: These can be assembled ahead of time and broiled just before serving.

Janica Paustian   **College Park High School, Pleasant Hill, CA**

Hot Parmesan Herb Bread

Serves 6 - 8

1 loaf sourdough bread, unsliced
$1/4$ to $1/2$ cup butter, softened
1 to 3 cloves garlic, minced
1 teaspoon parsley flakes
$1/2$ teaspoon oregano leaves, crumbled
$1/4$ teaspoon dill weed
Parmesan cheese, grated

Slice bread vertically into 1" slices. Don't slice all the way through. Blend together butter, garlic, parsley, oregano and dill weed. Spread butter mixture in between bread slices. Shape foil around the loaf, boat fashion, twisting ends and leaving the top open. Sprinkle top and in between slices liberally with Parmesan cheese. Bake at 400 degrees for 10 minutes, or until golden brown.

"Family and guests will love this savory bread.
Whenever I serve this, I'm asked for the recipe."
Janet Tingley   **Atascadero High School, Atascadero, CA**

NOTES & REMINDERS

Grilled Parmesan Toast

Serves 8
  $1/2$ cup butter or margarine, room temperature
  $1/4$ cup Parmesan cheese, grated
  2 tablespoons fresh parsley, chopped
  I loaf (about 12" x 4") Italian bread

In small bowl, blend butter, cheese and parsley. Cut bread vertically into 1 $1/2$" slices. Split each slice in half, taking care not to cut all the way through the crust. Spread insides of each bread piece with Parmesan butter. Wrap bread in heavy duty aluminum foil and place over medium coals for about 15 minutes.

Margo Olsen   **Amador Valley High School, Pleasanton, CA**

Aunt Lorrayne's Killer Cinnamon Rolls

Serves 6 - 10
  I package frozen bread dough, thawed
  $3/4$ cup brown sugar, divided
  2 teaspoons cinnamon
  I cup vanilla ice cream
  $1/2$ cup sugar
  $1/4$ cup margarine

Roll out one loaf into a rectangle. Sprinkle with $1/4$ cup brown sugar and cinnamon. Roll lengthwise. Cut into 2" rounds. Place in a greased 9" x 13" baking pan. In saucepan, melt ice cream with sugar, remaining $1/2$ cup brown sugar and margarine until sugars are dissolved; do not boil. Pour over rolls and bake at 350 degrees for 15 to 20 minutes.

"These are just the best! Lorrayne taught 40 years in a rural district
in South Dakota, often hauling water for students herself!"
Nanci Burkhart   **Hueneme High School, Oxnard, CA**

Grandma's Potato Pan Rolls

Makes 4 dozen

- $^{2}/_{3}$ cup shortening
- 4 tablespoons sugar
- 2 teaspoons salt
- 1 cup mashed potato, freshly cooked, cooled
- 2 eggs, well beaten
- 1 tablespoon yeast
- 1 $^{1}/_{2}$ cups warm water
- 7 cups flour (approximate)
- 1 cube butter or margarine, melted

Cream shortening, sugar and salt. Blend in mashed potato until smooth. In separate bowl, combine eggs and yeast. Stir in warm water. Blend with shortening/sugar mixture. Sift in flour, mixing until dough is not sticky. Roll out dough on floured board, about $^{3}/_{8}$" thick. Cut out circles using a floured cutter or an inverted cup. Dip in melted butter, fold, porterhouse style. Bake 15 to 20 minutes at 425 degrees.

"I am always begged to make my grandmother's delicious rolls for an occasion."

Joan Ward   **Isbell Middle School, Santa Paula, CA**

Best Baked Beans

Serves 10 - 12

- $^{1}/_{2}$ pound bacon
- 1 (medium) onion, chopped
- 1 pound ground beef
- 1 (large) can pork 'n beans
- 1 can butter beans, drained
- 1 can kidney beans, drained
- 2 tablespoons vinegar
- $^{3}/_{4}$ cup brown sugar
- 1 teaspoon prepared mustard
- $^{1}/_{2}$ cup catsup
- 1 teaspoon salt

Fry bacon until crisp; drain and crumble. Sauté onion in bacon grease; drain. Brown ground beef; drain excess fat. In a large casserole dish, stir together bacon, onion, ground beef, beans and remaining ingredients. Bake, covered at 350 degrees for 45 minutes. NOTE: You can cook these beans in a crock pot on low for 3 hours.

"This is an essential dish at all family picnics and barbecues."

Linda A. Stokes   **Riverton High School, Riverton, UT**

NOTES & REMINDERS

59

Sauces & Marinades
RELISH • SALSA

Barbecue Rub for Ribs

Makes 2 cups

    2 cups sugar
    1/4 cup paprika
    2 teaspoons chili seasoning
    1/2 teaspoon cayenne pepper
    2 tablespoons salt
    2 teaspoons black pepper
    I teaspoon garlic powder
    I teaspoon onion powder
    ribs, pork or beef, amount desired
    barbecue sauce, any kind

Combine first eight ingredients in a shaker or glass jar with lid. Shake until mixed well. To use on ribs, peel membrane off back of each slab of ribs. Rinse each slab with cold running water; dry. Shake seasoning "rub" and lightly coat both sides. Place ribs in oven at 350 degrees for 45 minutes to 1 hour, until meat has shrunk away from bone. Remove from oven and baste ribs with any type barbecue sauce. Return to oven for 5 minutes. Serve.

"I found the answer to great tasting ribs... any store barbecue sauce works well. I make up a double batch of this rub and keep it on hand."

Karen Tilson   **Poly High School, Riverside, CA**

Best BBQ Sauce

Makes 2 cups

    1/2 cup brown sugar
    1/2 cup white sugar
    1/2 cup red wine or grape juice
    1/4 cup vinegar
    I cup catsup
    2 cloves garlic, minced
    dash cinnamon
    dash nutmeg
    dash allspice
    I tablespoon minced onion
    I teaspoon dried mustard

Place all ingredients in a small saucepan; simmer 20 minutes. Use right away or store in covered jar in refrigerator for 2 to 3 weeks.

Microwave directions: Place all ingredients in a 2 quart microwave safe bowl. Cook high 2 to 3 minutes, or until bubbly.

"Great on pork. Parboil ribs, drain and grill.
Brush on sauce during last 10 minutes, turning often. Also good on ham."

Linda Hubbs   **Lone Pine High School, Lone Pine, CA**

Could Be "Tony Roma's" Barbecue Sauce

Makes 4 cups

2 $\frac{1}{2}$ cups catsup
1 $\frac{1}{4}$ cups tomato sauce
1 tablespoon prepared mustard
$\frac{1}{2}$ cup brown sugar
1 tablespoon black pepper
$\frac{1}{2}$ cup wine vinegar
2 $\frac{1}{2}$ tablespoons bottled steak sauce
$\frac{1}{2}$ teaspoon Tabasco sauce
3 tablespoons Worcestershire sauce
3 tablespoons soy sauce
$\frac{1}{4}$ cup onion, chopped
2 cloves garlic, chopped
1 $\frac{1}{2}$ tablespoons liquid smoke
1 $\frac{1}{2}$ teaspoons salt
5 ounces canned beef broth

Combine all ingredients in a saucepan. Bring to a boil, then reduce heat and simmer 1 $\frac{1}{2}$ hours. Store in refrigerator.

"A recipe given by Tony Roma many years ago on the Dinah Shore TV program."

Carol Goddard   **Alhambra High School, Alhambra, CA**

Easy Barbecue Sauce

Makes 1 $\frac{1}{4}$ cups

2 tablespoons brown sugar
2 tablespoons Worcestershire sauce
1 tablespoon dry mustard
$\frac{3}{4}$ cup vinegar
$\frac{1}{3}$ cup catsup
1 teaspoon salt
1 teaspoon paprika
dash pepper
1 clove garlic, minced

Combine all ingredients in saucepan and simmer about 15 minutes. Use to baste 2 pounds of ribs or 2 small chickens.

Ginger Raven   **Chico Junior High School, Chico, CA**

NOTES & REMINDERS

61

Diabetic BBQ Sauce

Makes 1 $\frac{1}{4}$ cups

I cup catsup
2 tablespoons sugar free maple syrup
I tablespoon red wine vinegar
I tablespoon mustard
$\frac{1}{2}$ teaspoon garlic powder
I tablespoon minced onion
I to 2 packets Equal, or to taste

Mix all ingredients except Equal, then add Equal until desired sweetness is achieved. Baste foods with sauce and use for dipping.

"Especially good on ribs. There is some sugar in the catsup, but this is a great way for diabetics to get that sugar-glaze taste to a barbecue without the calories and sugar."
Linda Winzenread   **Whittier High School, Whittier, CA**

Ida's Barbecue Sauce

Makes 1 cup

I (medium) onion, finely chopped
I clove garlic, minced
$\frac{1}{2}$ cup olive oil
2 tablespoons brown sugar
I tablespoon chili powder
2 teaspoons salt
I teaspoon dry mustard
I teaspoon paprika
dash cayenne
$\frac{1}{8}$ teaspoon thyme
$\frac{1}{8}$ teaspoon marjoram
$\frac{1}{2}$ cup + 2 tablespoons water, divided
2 (8 ounce) cans tomato sauce
$\frac{1}{2}$ cup lemon juice
2 drops liquid smoke

Sauté onion and garlic in olive oil until soft. Mix brown sugar, chili powder, salt, mustard, paprika, cayenne, thyme and marjoram to a paste with 2 tablespoons water. Stir into onion mixture. Add tomato sauce, lemon juice, remaining $\frac{1}{2}$ cup water and liquid smoke. Simmer 15 minutes. Brush on chicken during barbecuing.

"This barbecue sauce is especially fabulous used with chicken on the grill."
Jan Tuttle   **Mills High School, Millbrae, CA**

NOTES & REMINDERS

Texan Barbecue Sauce

Makes 3 cups

    1 (12 to 16 ounce) jar barbecue sauce
    $2/_3$ (12 ounce) can beer
    3 tablespoons brown sugar
    $1/_4$ cup vinegar
    2 to 3 dashes Worcestershire sauce
    dash Tabasco sauce

On stove top or in microwave, bring all ingredients to a boil. Turn off heat and cover. Use lavishly for beef or any barbecued meats.

"I picked up this recipe while visiting friends in Denton, Texas."

Deborah Scott-Toux   **Eisenhower High School, Rialto, CA**

BBQ Sauce for Salmon

Makes 2 cups

    1 cup butter
    1 $1/_2$ cups beer
    $2/_3$ cup brown sugar
    1 teaspoon liquid smoke

In a 4 cup measuring cup, melt butter in microwave. Add beer and brown sugar and blend. Add the liquid smoke. Grill salmon fillets or steaks on barbecue. The last 5 minutes of grilling, brush with sauce, on both sides. NOTE: I usually make a half of the recipe for a family dinner.

"This recipe comes from dear friends in Snohomish, WA, the Plags."

Sue Waterbury   **San Luis Obispo High School, San Luis Obispo, CA**

Luau Barbecue Sauce

Makes 2 cups

    2 cups strained peaches (baby food or pureed)
    $1/_3$ cup catsup
    $1/_3$ cup vinegar
    2 tablespoons soy sauce
    $1/_2$ cup brown sugar
    2 teaspoons ginger
    1 teaspoon salt
    dash pepper

Mix all ingredients together and use as a basting barbecue sauce for chicken or spare ribs.

"This is one of the favorite requested recipes from my mom's church cookbook."

Kris Haas   **West Jordan High School, West Jordan, UT**

Chicken Basting Sauce

Makes 2 cups

1 (5 ounce) bottle Worcestershire sauce ($^2/_3$ cup)
$^1/_2$ cup oil
$^1/_3$ cup lemon juice
1 clove garlic, minced

Combine all ingredients and use to baste your chicken while barbecuing.

Pam Cahill   **Eureka High School, Eureka, CA**

Captain Coon's Honey/Pineapple Glaze

Makes 2 cups

$^3/_4$ cup honey
$^1/_2$ cup Dijon mustard
1 cup pineapple juice (or crushed pineapple with juice)
2 tablespoons cornstarch
$^1/_4$ cup water

In a 2 quart saucepan on grill rack over coals, or over medium-high heat on stove, bring honey, mustard and pineapple juice or crushed pineapple with juice, to a boil. In a cup, blend cornstarch with water until smooth. Add to honey mixture, stirring constantly, until thickened. Grill meat for about 10 minutes, brush on glaze and cook through.

*"Sailed the 'Trilogy' on our honeymoon from Maui to Lanai
and were served this glaze on chicken for lunch. It's still a favorite!"*

Connie Sweet   **Rim of the World High School, Lake Arrowhead, CA**

Dry Marinade for Scrumptious Meats

Makes 1 cup

2 tablespoons dried rosemary, crumbled
2 tablespoons dried thyme, crumbled
1 bay leaf, crumbled
$^1/_2$ head garlic, cloves peeled (or more to taste)
$^1/_4$ cup olive oil
3 tablespoons Dijon mustard
1 $^1/_2$ teaspoons ground coriander
1 teaspoon cayenne pepper
freshly ground pepper
meat of your choice

Grind rosemary, thyme and bay leaf in food processor. With machine running, add peeled garlic cloves through feed tube and mince. Add all remaining ingredients, except meat, and puree until it becomes a paste. Place meat in glass baking dish. Rub with paste. Cover and refrigerate overnight. Next day, barbecue as usual.

"An elegant crowd pleaser. My husband likes this rub on lamb."

Jan Schulenburg   **Irvine High School, Irvine, CA**

Grilled
Vegetable Platter
SIDE DISHES.....PAGE 56

Cheese-Stuffed Burgers
MAIN DISHES.....PAGE 87

Grilled Chicken and Pasta Salad
MAIN DISHES.....PAGE 83

Easy 1, 2, 3 Marinade
Makes 2 cups
>   1 ¹/₂ cups red wine
>   ³/₄ cup soy sauce
>   garlic, minced

Combine red wine and soy sauce; set aside. Rub minced garlic on both sides of meat. Pour marinade over meat. Cover and refrigerate at least 4 hours. Turn meat halfway through marinating time. NOTE: This is a great marinade for flank steak.

"We take this river rafting every summer. Just place the meat and marinade in a freezer ziploc bag and place it in the cooler. Or freeze it prior."

Ann Mohr   **Cyprus High School, Magna, UT**

Easy, But Great Marinade
Makes 2 cups
>   1 cup cola or lemon lime soda
>   1 cup soy sauce or teriyaki sauce

Pour soda and sauce into a ziploc bag. Add desired meat or poultry; seal and refrigerate at least 4 to 6 hours. Drain and barbecue.

"Easy and amazingly good. I got this recipe at a little league ball field."

Karol A. Meryhew   **Granger High School, West Valley, UT**

Flank Steak Marinade
Serves 3 - 4
>   ¹/₂ cup pineapple juice
>   1 cup soy sauce
>   ¹/₂ cup vinegar
>   ¹/₂ cup brown sugar
>   1 teaspoon garlic powder OR 1 clove fresh garlic, chopped
>   2 to 3 pounds flank steak

In a small saucepan, bring pineapple juice, soy sauce, vinegar, brown sugar and garlic to a boil, then lower heat and simmer 5 to 10 minutes, stirring occasionally. Let marinade cool. Score flank steak lightly on both sides. Place in a large ziploc bag and pour cooled marinade over steak. Refrigerate at least 2 hours, or overnight, rotating every few hours. When ready to serve, grill or broil 5 minutes on medium heat on each side; do not overcook. Cut into thin slices and serve.

"This is so easy and a very big hit with family and friends. The longer you marinate, the better. Great leftovers for tortillas or stir fry."

Ruth Anne Mills   **Los Alisos Intermediate School, Mission Viejo, CA**

NOTES & REMINDERS

Quick Barbecue Marinade

Makes 1 cup

2 cloves garlic minced or pressed
2 tablespoons olive or salad oil
$1/4$ teaspoon dry mustard
1 teaspoon soy sauce
$1/4$ teaspoon dried rosemary
2 tablespoons wine vinegar
$1/4$ cup dry white wine
$1/4$ teaspoon Worcestershire sauce
1 $1/2$ teaspoons meat seasoning sauce

Cook garlic in oil over low heat just until softened, do not brown. Add mustard, soy sauce and rosemary. Remove from heat and stir in vinegar, wine, Worcestershire and seasoning sauce. Pour over meat, cover and refrigerate until next day, turning occasionally.

Pat Peck   **Folsom High School, Folsom, CA**

Oberia's Marinade

Makes 1 cup

$1/2$ cup wine, any type
3 to 5 drops liquid smoke
$1/2$ cup soy sauce
1 teaspoon garlic powder
1 tablespoon dried minced onions

Combine all ingredients in a large measuring cup. Use to marinate meat, cut into serving size pieces. Cover and refrigerate at least 12 hours. Barbecue and enjoy. NOTE: This works great with pork tenderloin, tri-tip, pork chops and steaks. The recipe may be easily doubled or tripled.

"A friend of my mother's, who worked at Beale Air Force Base Commissary, was kind enough to share this recipe with our family."

DeLisa Davis   **Sutter High School, Sutter, CA**

Kabob Marinade

Makes 1 cup

$1/2$ cup olive oil
$1/2$ cup wine vinegar
1 teaspoon salt
1 teaspoon marjoram
1 teaspoon thyme
$1/2$ teaspoon pepper
1 clove garlic, minced
$1/2$ cup onion, chopped
$1/4$ cup parsley, snipped
juice of $1/2$ lemon

Combine all ingredients. Marinate desired meat at least 24 hours. This marinade is enough for 2 to 3 pounds of kabob meat (chicken, beef or lamb). Best cooked over charcoal.

Judy Dobkins   **Redlands High School, Redlands, CA**

Seattle Steak Marinade

Serves 4

$1/2$ teaspoon pepper
$1/2$ teaspoon lemon pepper
$1/2$ teaspoon seasoning salt
1 tablespoon minced onion
1 clove garlic, minced
$1/4$ teaspoon crushed red pepper
$1/4$ teaspoon garlic salt
$1/4$ teaspoon oregano
$1/4$ teaspoon sage, ground or crushed
$3/4$ cup Italian salad dressing

Poke both sides of meat with a fork and sprinkle pepper, lemon pepper and seasoning salt on both sides. Mix minced onion with garlic, along with spices, herbs and Italian dressing in a plastic ziploc bag. Place meat inside and turn over several times to coat. Place on a dish and marinate 2 to 4 hours, or overnight. Grill as desired.

"This is my husband's specialty!
This is passed on from a Seattle Coastie (U.S. Coast Guard) shipmate."

Debra Jamison   **Sierra Vista High School, Las Vegas, NV**

NOTES & REMINDERS

Teriyaki Sauce Marinade

Makes 3 cups

> 1 cup soy sauce
> 1 cup sugar
> 1 teaspoon fresh ginger
> 1 teaspoon fresh garlic
> pinch salt
> 2 tablespoons brown sugar
> 1 1/2 cups water
> 1/2 cup cornstarch

Combine soy sauce, sugar, ginger, garlic, salt, brown sugar and water; mix well. Add cornstarch to thicken sauce. Marinate any meat at least one hour. Grill on barbecue.

"My three boys say it's the best marinade in the world. It's requested at every barbecue. Set aside some marinade to brush on meat as it cooks."

Cheryl M. Moyle   **Olympus High School, Salt Lake City, UT**

Healthy Teriyaki Sauce

Makes 1 quart

> 2 cups soy sauce
> 1/2 cup pineapple juice
> 3 tablespoons molasses
> 3 cloves garlic, minced (or more if you like garlic)
> 1/4 cup fresh ginger, peeled, sliced
> 3 green onions, chopped

In a 2 quart cooking pot, bring all ingredients to a boil, reduce heat and simmer until mixture is thickened, about 10 to 20 minutes. Watch out for boil over; do not leave sauce unattended. Strain into container for later use, or pour into large bowl or Tupperware holding meat or tofu. Marinate at least 2 hours; a few days is even better! Barbecue marinated product. Watch for flare ups on barbecue, due to sugar content.

"No processed sugar. Molasses will provide a source of iron! This recipe can be enlarged to make gallons instead of a quart."

Victoria Star   **C.K.McClatchy High School, Sacramento, CA**

Teriyaki Sake Sauce

Serves 4 - 6

> 1/2 cup Shoyu soy sauce
> 1/4 cup sake
> 2 (small) pieces ginger root, peeled, sliced
> 2 green onions, chopped
> 1 tablespoon sugar
> 1 tablespoon brown sugar
> 1 (small) clove garlic, crushed

Mix together all ingredients in a glass baking dish. Add steak or chicken and marinate in sauce 24 hours, then grill.

"This is an Alfafara family recipe from Hawaii."

Janet Alfafara **Ontario High School, Ontario, CA**

Mom Orashen's Relish

Makes 8 pints

4 (large) onions, peeled
1 (medium) cabbage
10 green tomatoes, cored
12 green peppers, cored
6 red peppers, cored
$1/2$ cup salt
1 $1/2$ teaspoons turmeric
2 cups water
6 cups sugar
1 tablespoon celery seed
2 tablespoons mustard seed
4 cups cider vinegar

Grind vegetables; sprinkle with $1/2$ cup salt and let stand overnight. Rinse and drain. Combine remaining ingredients and pour over vegetables. Heat to boiling. Simmer 3 minutes. Pour into hot sterilized jars and seal.

"Not a typical relish! It's worth the effort. My husband can't live without it!"

Dale Sheehan **Santana High School, Santee, CA**

Mango Salsa

Serves 4 - 6

$1/2$ red onion, finely chopped
$1/2$ bunch fresh cilantro, finely chopped
juice of 1 lime
2 mangos, peeled, seeded, diced
salt and pepper, to taste

Toss ingredients together. Serve with barbecued fish.

"From my friend, Joyce Dickinson. This fruit salsa is wonderful over barbecued fish. My favorite is salmon. Try substituting oranges or pineapple for the mango."

Pat Hufnagel **Esperanza High School, Anaheim, CA**

NOTES & REMINDERS

Orange Sauce for Fruit

Makes 1 cup

$1/4$ cup sugar
1 tablespoon cornstarch
$1/2$ cup water
$1/2$ cup orange juice
1 teaspoon butter
pinch salt
$1/2$ teaspoon orange rind (optional)

In a saucepan, cook sugar, cornstarch, water and orange juice over low heat until clear, stirring constantly. Remove from heat and add butter, salt and orange rind, if using. Stir and chill. Pour over fruit prior to serving.

"Wonderful over a mixed melon salad. We use watermelon, cantaloupe, honeydew and even strawberries sometimes. From my mom, Minnie's kitchen!"

Maria Fregulia   **Lassen High School, Susanville, CA**

Barbecued Chicken

Serves 4

$1/4$ cup reduced sodium catsup
3 tablespoons cider vinegar
1 tablespoon prepared white horseradish
2 teaspoons dark brown sugar, firmly packed
1 clove garlic, minced
$1/8$ teaspoon dried thyme
$1/4$ teaspoon black pepper
4 skinless boneless chicken breast halves

Prepare grill for barbecuing. Turn gas grill to medium, or prepare charcoal. In a small saucepan, combine catsup, vinegar, horseradish, brown sugar, garlic and thyme; mix well. Bring to a boil over medium-low heat. Cook, stirring frequently until thickened, about 5 minutes. Remove from heat and stir in pepper. Brush tops of chicken lightly with sauce. Place chicken, sauce side down, on a grill rack. Brush other sides lightly with sauce. Grill 3" from heat, basting with remaining sauce and turning until no longer pink in center, about 5 to 7 minutes per side. Let chicken stand 5 minutes before serving.

"Have a great meal in about 30 minutes!"

Sally Engel   **Elsinore Middle School, Lake Elsinore, CA**

71

Chicken Charlena

Serves 10

> 10 boneless, skinless chicken breasts
> 5 to 6 cloves garlic, pureed
> $1/4$ cup dried oregano
> salt and pepper, to taste
> $1/2$ cup red wine vinegar
> $1/2$ cup olive oil
> 1 cup figs
> 1 cup pitted prunes
> $1/2$ cup Spanish olives, pitted
> $1/2$ cup capers, with small amount of juice
> 6 bay leaves
> 1 cup brown sugar
> 1 cup white wine
> $1/4$ cup fresh cilantro, finely chopped

Cut chicken breasts in half lengthwise and pound until $1/2$" thick. Place in single layer in 9" x 13" glass baking dish or casserole dish. In large bowl, mix together garlic, oregano, salt, pepper, vinegar, olive oil, figs, prunes, olives, capers with juice, and bay leaves. Spoon marinade over chicken. Cover and let marinate overnight in refrigerator. Next day, allow pans to come to room temperature. Preheat oven to 350 degrees. Sprinkle chicken with brown sugar and pour white wine around. Bake, uncovered for 1 hour at 350 degrees, or until juice runs clear when poked with fork. Baste frequently with sauce. When done, transfer chicken, olives, figs, prunes and capers to a serving platter using a slotted spoon. Moisten with a little of the juice and pour the remaining juice into a gravy boat. Serve with chicken, if desired.

"This is also great cold! It is a favorite for potluck, because it's a one-dish meal. Thanks to my Bunco friend, Lisa Panacci, for sharing this recipe with me."

Charlene Nugent   **Petaluma Junior High School, Petaluma, CA**

Chicken-N-Que Sauce

Serves 8

> 4 chickens, cut in half
> oil, for brushing chicken
> $1/2$ cup salad oil
> $3/4$ cup lemon juice
> $1/4$ cup white wine
> 3 tablespoons sugar
> 1 tablespoon + 1 $1/2$ teaspoons salt

Wash and dry chicken halves. Brush with salad oil. Brown over coals on barbecue grill, turning as necessary. Heat remaining ingredients to boiling. Cook until sugar is dissolved. Place each browned chicken half on foil, divide sauce over chicken pieces, seal tightly and cook on grill without moving, 45 minutes or until done.

"This very old recipe is a barbecue favorite of my husband's family."

Judy Herman   **Dublin High School, Dublin, CA**

Corn & Salsa Chicken Packets

Serves 4

    4 sheets (12" x 18") heavy duty aluminum foil
    4 boneless, skinless chicken breast halves (1 to 1 $^1/_4$ pounds)
    1 cup chunky salsa
    1 (10 ounce) package frozen whole kernel corn
      OR 1 (15.25 ounce) can whole kernel corn, drained
    1 cup cheddar cheese, shredded

Preheat oven to 450 degrees or grill to medium-high. Center one chicken breast half on each sheet of heavy duty aluminum foil. Spoon salsa over chicken. Top with corn. Bring up foil sides. Double fold top and ends to seal packet, leaving room for heat circulation inside. Repeat to make four packets. Bake 18 to 22 minutes on cookie sheet or grill 12 to 15 minutes in covered grill. After cooking, open end of foil packet first to allow steam to escape. Then open top of foil packet. Sprinkle with cheese before serving.

Patty Stroming   **Mitchell Sr. Elementary, Atwater, CA**

Barbecued Asian Chicken

Serves 6

    $^1/_4$ cup vegetable oil
    3 tablespoons hot chili sauce
    2 tablespoons honey
    1 tablespoon paprika
    7 green onions
    6 boneless, skinless chicken breast halves
    salt

Whisk oil, chili sauce, honey and paprika in a pie plate to blend. (You may substitute part of the vegetable oil with hot chili oil if desired.) Mince only one of the green onions and add to marinade. Remove $^1/_2$ cup marinade and set aside. In remaining marinade, marinate chicken for 2 hours. Prepare barbecue. Sprinkle chicken and remaining onions with salt. Barbecue chicken until cooked through and onions are softened, turning occasionally, approximately 10 to 20 minutes. Transfer to plate and drizzle with remaining $^1/_2$ cup marinade.

"This is spicy! Some of my students made it in lab and loved it!
It's different from your usual marinades!"

Wendy Barnes   **Vasquez High School, Acton, CA**

NOTES & REMINDERS

73

Cuban Chicken

Serves 4 - 6

2 pounds chicken, cut up, or breast meat, with ribs attached
  (not boneless chicken breasts as they will dry out)
2 tablespoons oil
1 can chicken broth
1 (14.5 ounce) can diced tomatoes
$1/3$ cup water
$1/2$ cup onion, chopped
2 cloves garlic, minced
1 teaspoon salt
1 teaspoon turmeric or saffron
$1/8$ teaspoon pepper
1 bay leaf
10 ounces frozen peas
1 cup short grain rice (not converted rice)
$1/4$ to $1/2$ cup whole stuffed green olives

Brown chicken in oil. Add broth, tomatoes, water, onion, garlic, salt, turmeric or saffron, pepper and bay leaf. Cover and cook over low heat for 15 minutes. Add peas, rice and olives. Cover and cook about 30 minutes more on low heat. Remove from heat when chicken is tender.

"Don't let the ingredient list stop you. It's a pretty quick and easy recipe.
Growing up, I was the envy of other kids when I got called to dinner."

Pat Hufnagel   **Esperanza High School, Anaheim, CA**

Indonesian Chicken Breasts

Serves 4

$1/2$ cup orange juice
$1/4$ cup peanut butter
2 teaspoons curry powder
4 boneless, skinless chicken breasts
1 (medium) red bell pepper, cut in half, sliced into $1/2$" strips
$1/4$ cup coconut, shredded
$1/4$ cup currants or raisins
2 cups rice, cooked

Beat orange juice, peanut butter and curry powder in medium non-metal bowl, using wire whisk. Add chicken, turning to coat with marinade. Cover and refrigerate, turning once, at least 1 hour. Heat coals or gas grill. Remove chicken from marinade; discard marinade. Grill chicken 15 to 20 minutes over medium coals or heat. To serve, cut chicken breast diagonally into $1/2$" slices . Top with sliced bell pepper, coconut and currants or raisins. Serve with rice.

Julie Daters   **Summerville High School, Tuolumne, CA**

NOTES & REMINDERS

Italian Stallion Chicken Barbecue

Serves 4

> 4 chicken breast halves, boneless, skinless
> 1 (8 ounce) bottle Italian dressing

Marinate chicken in Italian dressing overnight. Heat grill to high. Place chicken on grill, lower temperature and turn over when seared. Cook until done, approximately 5 minutes more.

> *"Serve with fresh green salad, corn on the cob and baked potato.*
> *Excellent summer meal, healthy, and low calorie! Yum!"*

Teresa Stahl   **Needles High School, Needles, CA**

NOTES & REMINDERS

Cumin Chicken

Serves 4

> 4 cloves garlic, minced
> 1 1/2 teaspoons ground cumin
> 1 1/2 cups pineapple juice
> 4 boneless, skinless chicken breasts

In an oblong glass baking dish, stir together garlic, ground cumin and pineapple juice, stirring until cumin is completely dissolved. Pierce chicken breasts with a fork on both sides. Marinate in juice for 2 to 24 hours in refrigerator. Remove from refrigerator 30 minutes before cooking. Barbecue or broil for 5 minutes on each side, or until cooked through.

> *"Great as an entreé with rice and vegetables or as taco or enchilada filling."*

Leslie Corsini   **Nicolas Junior High School, Fullerton, CA**

Grilled Lemon-Mustard Chicken

Serves 6

> *Marinade:*
> 1/2 cup lemon juice
> 1 tablespoon lemon zest
> 1/4 cup Dijon mustard
> 1/4 cup fresh herbs (any combination of rosemary, thyme, basil,
>   oregano, parsley), finely chopped
> 3/4 teaspoon salt
> 1/4 teaspoon pepper
> 4 whole chicken breasts, skinned, boned, halved
> *Garnish:* Parsley sprigs, lemon slices, fresh herbs

Combine marinade ingredients in non-aluminum dish or bowl. Add chicken pieces, turning to coat evenly with marinade. Cover and refrigerate for 2 hours to overnight. Prepare barbecue for medium-heat grilling. Remove chicken from marinade and grill for 8 minutes on each side. Place on platter surrounded by desired garnishes.

> *"Easy to expand ingredients for a party using drumsticks, thighs and wings.*
> *This is a fresh alternative to a tomato based sauce."*

Toni Morucci   **Oroville High School, Oroville, CA**

Grilled Chicken Cordon Bleu

Serves 6

>   6 boneless skinless chicken breasts
>   6 slices Swiss cheese
>   6 slices deli-style ham
>   3 tablespoons olive or vegetable oil
> $^3/_4$ cup seasoned bread crumbs

Flatten chicken to $^1/_4$" thickness. Place a slice of cheese and slice of ham on each flattened breast to within $^1/_4$" of edges. Fold in half and secure with thin metal skewer or toothpicks. Brush with oil and roll in bread crumbs. Grill, covered, over medium-hot heat for 15 to 18 minutes or until juices run clear when pierced.

"You can assemble these early and leave in refrigerator up to 8 hours."
Gale Hooper   **Casa Roble High School, Orangevale, CA**

Grilled Chicken with Wine Sauce

Serves 4

> $^1/_2$ cup butter or margarine, melted
> $^1/_4$ cup dry white wine
>   1 tablespoon lemon juice
>   2 tablespoons soy sauce
>   1 teaspoon garlic powder
>   1 teaspoon onion powder
>   1 teaspoon paprika
> $^1/_2$ teaspoon tarragon
>   1 frying chicken, cut into pieces

Combine butter or margarine, wine, lemon juice, soy sauce, garlic powder, onion powder, paprika and tarragon; mix well. Grill chicken pieces over hot coals until tender, about 35 to 40 minutes, turning occasionally. Baste chicken frequently with the sauce mixture.

"This is a great recipe for last minute guests."
Wanda Shelton   **Newport Harbor HS, Newport Beach, CA**

Grilled Spicy Marinated Chicken

Serves 8

2 cups green onions or scallions, finely chopped
2 Scotch Bonnet or habanero chilies, seeded, minced
   OR I tablespoons Scotch Bonnet Pepper sauce
2 tablespoons soy sauce
2 tablespoons fresh lime juice
5 teaspoons ground allspice
3 teaspoons English-style dry mustard (Coleman's)
2 bay leaves, center ribs discarded, leaves crumbled
2 cloves garlic, chopped
I tablespoon salt
2 teaspoons sugar
I $^1/_2$ teaspoons dried thyme, crushed
I teaspoon cinnamon
5 pounds chicken parts, (remove wing tips)
oil for brushing the grill

Combine all ingredients except chicken and oil in a food processor or blender and puree. Divide chicken parts between two heavy duty ziploc bags. Pour marinade evenly over both. Coat chicken well and press out excess air; seal. Put bags in refrigerator for two days, turning several times. (Minimum time to marinate is 24 hours.) Preheat grill, brush with oil and place chicken over hot coals, about 4 to 6 inches above coals. Cook in batches, if necessary, and covered, if possible for about 10 to 15 minutes on each side or until cooked through. Place on heated platter and keep warm until ready to serve.

"This is the best tasting barbecue chicken ever! It has a Caribbean flavor that's just right. If you want it hotter, add more chiles."
Sandra Massey   **Mountain View High School, El Monte, CA**

Grilled Teriyaki Chicken

Serves 4

4 boneless, skinless chicken breasts
I cup teriyaki sauce
$^1/_4$ cup lemon juice
2 teaspoons garlic, grated
2 teaspoons sesame oil

Place chicken, teriyaki sauce, lemon juice, garlic and sesame oil in a large ziploc bag. Seal bag and shake to coat. Place in refrigerator for 24 hours, turning several times. Preheat gill for medium high heat and lightly oil grate. Remove chicken from bag, discarding remaining marinade. Grill 6 to 8 minutes on each side.

"This is the best chicken you'll ever taste! Just be careful when making it for friends. They'll want you to make it all the time!"
Natalie Henwood   **Riverton High School, Riverton, UT**

77

Caribbean Teriyaki Skewers

Serves 4 - 6   *Photo opposite page 97*

> 1 ³/₄ pounds boneless, skinless chicken breasts,
>   cut into chunks, divided
> 1 (12 ounce) bottle Lawry's Caribbean Jerk Marinade with Papaya Juice
> ³/₄ pound sirloin steak, cut into chunks
> 1 (12 ounce) bottle Lawry's Teriyaki Marinade with
>   Pineapple Juice, divided
> 15 (medium) shrimp, peeled and deveined
> Wooden skewers

In a large ziploc bag, combine 1 pound chicken chunks with ²/₃ cup Caribbean Jerk Marinade; seal thoroughly and shake to coat. In another large ziploc bag, combine remaining chicken cubes and sirloin cubes with 1 cup Teriyaki Marinade; seal thoroughly and shake to coat. Marinate both meats 30 minutes in refrigerator. Remove from refrigerator and discard used marinade. Thread jerk marinated chicken cubes onto skewers. Thread shrimp onto skewers. Thread teriyaki marinated chicken and steak onto skewers. Grill or broil 10 to 15 minutes, rotating skewers and basting with remaining marinade often. Cook until chicken is no longer pink and juices run clear; add steak and shrimp and cook to desired doneness. Use remaining marinade to baste often while cooking. Serve with remaining marinades as a dipping sauce.

"Thanks goes to Eileen M. Jaynes of Lawry's Foods for this recipe."

Lawry's Foods, Inc.   **Monrovia, CA**

Lowfat Chicken Kabobs

Serves 4

> 2 tablespoons brown sugar
> 2 cloves garlic, minced
> ¹/₄ cup soy sauce
> ¹/₄ cup ground ginger
> 4 chicken breasts, cut into 1" cubes
> 1 (large) green pepper, cut into 1" pieces
> 1 (large) onion, cut into 1" wedges
> 1 can pineapple chunks, drained
> 12 (large) mushrooms

Combine brown sugar with garlic, soy sauce and ginger. Put cubed chicken in a large ziploc bag and pour marinade over to coat. Refrigerate at least 2 hours or overnight. When ready to cook, skewer the meat, alternating with green peppers, onions, pineapple and mushrooms. Broil in oven 3 minutes, turning over once and broiling 2 to 3 minutes longer or barbecue over hot coals, turning occasionally, until chicken is cooked through. NOTE: Beef may be substituted for chicken.

Janet Dukes   **Newport Harbor High School, Newport Beach, CA**

NOTES & REMINDERS

Barbecue Chicken Teriyaki

Serves 4 - 6

  8 boneless, skinless chicken breast halves
  1 cup soy sauce
  $^3/_4$ cup sugar
  $^1/_4$ cup sweet rice wine
  $^1/_2$ teaspoon ginger, minced
  $^1/_2$ teaspoon garlic, minced

Place chicken in a baking pan. Mix soy sauce, sugar, rice wine, ginger and garlic in a bowl. Pour over chicken. Bake at 375 degrees: If using frozen chicken, bake 1 hour, 10 minutes; if using fresh chicken, bake 45 minutes, until cooked through. If barbecuing chicken, bake chicken first without marinade, then barbecue to heat through. Boil marinade and serve with chicken.

"We take this camping. After baking, cool chicken, then freeze in ziploc freezer bag. At camp, we barbecue the chicken to heat through, then serve with marinade. Using frozen chicken keeps the chicken moist."

Reiko Ikkanda   **So. Pasadena Middle School, So. Pasadena, CA**

Split-Grilled Cornish Game Hens

Serves 2 - 4

  2 Cornish game hens
  3 to 4 tablespoons olive oil
  3 to 4 tablespoons Dijon mustard
  salt and pepper, to taste

Clean and split through breasts of game hens. Remove any protruding bones, especially ribs. Rub skin and meat sides with olive oil and Dijon mustard. Salt and pepper to taste. Allow to marinate at least 1 hour. On medium-low grill, place hens skin-side down and grill approximately 7 minutes per side, turning only 1 or 2 times, being careful not to overcook as they will become dry. Use a meat thermometer (165 degrees) if necessary.

"This is a great alternative to the everyday barbecue chicken meal."

Delaine Smith   **West Valley High School, Cottonwood, CA**

NOTES & REMINDERS

Beer Butt Chicken

Serves 2 - 4

Memphis Rub:

2 tablespoons paprika (Spanish Pimiento is really good)
1 $\frac{1}{2}$ teaspoons dark brown sugar
1 $\frac{1}{2}$ teaspoons sugar
1 teaspoon salt
1 teaspoon cayenne pepper
$\frac{1}{2}$ teaspoon celery salt
$\frac{1}{2}$ teaspoon dry mustard
$\frac{1}{2}$ teaspoon garlic powder
$\frac{1}{2}$ teaspoon onion powder
1 (medium) whole chicken, wing tips tucked in
2 $\frac{1}{2}$ tablespoons Memphis Rub
1 can beer, room temperature

Combine all ingredients for Memphis rub; mixing well. Rinse chicken inside and out; pat dry. Wash the beer can with soap and water. Rinse and dry. Sprinkle 1 tablespoon of Rub inside the chicken. Rub 1 tablespoon Rub on the skin. Open beer can , then using a church key type opener, make 5 to 6 holes in top of the can. Pour out the top inch of beer from can and spoon in the remaining Rub. Set beer can on counter and place chicken's butt over the can so that the can is almost completely hidden inside the chicken. Set the can and chicken on the grill, cover grill and cook for about 1 $\frac{1}{2}$ hours on medium heat, until chicken is done. NOTE: You may use nonalcoholic beer, if desired.

"This tastes pretty good; it's a beautiful color, but really a weird cooking method. This method makes the chicken a perfectly browned even color."

Sandy Massey   **Mountain View High School, El Monte, CA**

Tangy Apricot Chicken

Serves 4

1 cup barbecue sauce
1 cup apricot jam
4 boneless, skinless chicken breasts

Combine barbecue sauce with jam. Pour it over chicken in an electric skillet or oven proof dish. Bake at 350 degrees for 20 to 25 minutes. Use the sauce that is left in the pan for a dipping sauce.

"My kids love this recipe. It sounds weird, but it is so easy and tastes great!"

Kathy Sandoz   **Mesa Junior High School, Mesa, AZ**

Sweet Barbecue Chicken

Serves (an amount up to you)
Chicken
Barbecue Sauce
1 can crushed pineapple

Place chicken in crock pot. Cover with barbecue sauce and pineapple. Cook on high for about 5 hours.

Debi Spencer **Colton High School, Colton, CA**

Cajun Stew

Serves 8
6 chicken thighs, skinned
1 tablespoon oil
1 package turkey kielbasa sausage
1 pound ham, cut into cubes
1 (12 ounce) can hominy
2 cans stewed tomatoes
1 can black beans
1 (medium) onion, chopped
2 cups mushrooms, sliced
1 teaspoon white pepper
1 teaspoon black pepper
1 teaspoon red pepper
1 teaspoon gumbo file
1 teaspoon thyme
chicken broth, if needed
2 cups instant rice (optional)
chicken broth, if needed for moisture

Lightly sauté chicken thighs in oil. Stir in kielbasa and ham and continue sautéing. Add hominy, tomatoes, black beans, onion, mushrooms and spices. Stew 2 to 4 hours on low heat, adding chicken stock if mixture becomes too dry. The longer you cook it, the better it tastes. Stir in instant rice 20 to 30 minutes before serving, if desired. NOTE: This works nicely in a crockpot.

"From our school Librarian, Tom Vlahos. You can add or delete items, as available. This is a 'clean out your freezer' type dish."

Mary Springhorn **Anderson High School, Anderson, CA**

All American BBQ Chicken Wrap

Serves 1

1 chicken breast, grilled
1 ear corn, grilled
1 spinach or tomato tortilla
1 ounce mayonnaise
6 ounces mashed potatoes
1 cup romaine lettuce, torn into bite-sized pieces
1 ounce barbecue sauce

Cut grilled chicken breast into julienne strips. Shuck grilled corn and cut corn from cob. Place tortilla on the griddle to warm for 30 seconds. Remove from heat and spread with mayonnaise, then place mashed potatoes down center. Top with grilled chicken, corn and romaine lettuce. Drizzle with barbecue sauce, then roll up into shape of burrito. Wrap in foil and cut in half. Serve with desired garnishes.

Maria Hoffman   **Katella High School, Anaheim, CA**

Lime Chicken Fajitas

Serves 6

1 1/2 pounds boneless skinless chicken breasts
juice of 4 limes
2 tablespoons + 1/4 cup olive oil, divided
1 teaspoon dried oregano
1 teaspoon coarsely ground black pepper, divided
1 teaspoon salt, divided
2 (large) yellow onions, cut into 1/4" slivers
12 corn tortillas
1 cup guacamole, prepared
8 ounces plain yogurt
2 plum tomatoes, diced
1 tablespoon parsley, chopped

In a glass bowl, place chicken breasts in lime juice, 2 tablespoons olive oil, oregano, 1/2 teaspoon pepper and 1/2 teaspoon salt for 2 hours. In a shallow roasting pan, combine slivered onions with chicken and marinade. Cover with foil and bake 15 to 20 minutes at 350 degrees. Transfer onions to a heavy skillet with remaining 1/4 cup olive oil. Add pan juices, and remaining 1/2 teaspoon salt and pepper. Cook over medium heat for 15 minutes, stirring often, until onions are very soft and slightly browned. Drain excess liquid. Place chicken on grill and cook about 2 minutes on each side. Slice into strips 3" long by 1/2" wide. Place chicken in center of each tortilla with onions, a dollop of guacamole, yogurt and tomatoes. Sprinkle each with chopped parsley. Fold or roll to serve.

"This is one of my husband, Bill's, best recipes. Delicious with fresh tortillas."

Mary M. Rector   **Valley High School, Las Vegas, NV**

NOTES & REMINDERS

82

Grilled Chicken & Pasta Shells Salad

Serves 4   *Photo opposite page 65*

    $1/2$ (I pound) package Prince Medium Shells, cooked as package directs
    2 (medium) tomatoes, chopped
    4 ounces feta cheese, crumbled
    I (8 ounce) bottle Italian salad dressing
    2 cups torn leaf lettuce
    I pound boneless skinless chicken breast halves, grilled or broiled, sliced
    Parmesan cheese, grated (optional)

In a large bowl, combine cooked shells with tomatoes, feta cheese and salad dressing;
mix well. Cover and chill thoroughly. Just before serving, stir in lettuce, arrange
chicken on top. Serve with Parmesan cheese, if desired.

"This recipe comes from Sue Failor at Borden Foods."

Borden Foods Corp.   **Columbus, OH**

Chicken Casserole

Serves 12

    2 cups chicken, cooked
    2 cups rice, cooked
    2 cups celery, chopped
    4 tablespoons onion, chopped
    2 cans cream of chicken soup
    I $1/2$ cups mayonnaise
    2 cups water chestnuts, chopped
    I package Stove Top stuffing
    3 ounces butter or margarine, melted

Mix together chicken, rice, celery, onion, soup, mayonnaise and water chestnuts;
place in a 9" x 13" greased casserole. Top with dry stuffing mix; drizzle with butter.
Bake at 350 degrees for 45 minutes.

"A favorite potluck dish. I first tasted this at a church social in 1985."

Margaret McLeod   **Nogales High School, La Puente, CA**

Chicken Chalupa

Serves 6 - 8

    12 corn tortillas
    6 chicken breasts, cooked, diced
    I can mushroom soup
    I (large) can green chiles, diced
    I cup sour cream
    I (large) onion, chopped
    2 cups cheddar cheese, grated

Line the bottom of a 9" x 13" casserole with cut up pieces of corn tortillas. Combine
chicken with soup, green chiles, sour cream and onion. Spread half of this mixture

NOTES & REMINDERS

83

over tortillas. Cover with another layer of tortillas, a layer of chicken mixture, a layer of cheese and repeat, ending with cheese on top. Bake 45 minutes to 1 hour, at 350 degrees.

"Excellent recipe - my family loves it. It is one of their favorites!"

Olga Sarouhan   **Edison High School, Huntington Beach, CA**

Curry Chicken & Rice Casserole

Serves 8 - 10

> 2 cans cream of mushroom soup
> 1 cup mayonnaise
> 1 1/2 teaspoons curry powder
> 6 boneless skinless chicken breasts, cooked, cubed
> 2 boxes frozen chopped broccoli
> 1 (small) package frozen petite peas
> 3 cups rice, cooked
> paprika, to taste

Thoroughly mix soup, mayonnaise and curry powder. Partially defrost broccoli; drain any excess moisture. Mix all ingredients together and place in a 9" x 13" pan (there may be enough for an additional 8" x 8" pan). Top with a light sprinkle of paprika. Bake at 350 degrees for 45 to 50 minutes.

"Wonderful with a green salad and French bread."

Gail McAuley   **Lincoln High School, Stockton, CA**

Chili Chicken

Serves 12

> 16 ounces uncooked noodles
> 1/2 cup onion, chopped
> 2 tablespoons butter
> 3 (10.5 ounce) cans condensed cream of mushroom soup
> 1 (4 ounce) can pimiento, chopped
> 2 tablespoons hot green chili peppers, chopped
> 4 cups chicken, cooked
> salt and pepper, to taste
> 3 cups sharp cheddar cheese, shredded

Heat oven to 350 degrees. Cook noodles as directed on package; drain. In large skillet, cook and stir onion in butter until tender; stir in soup, pimiento and chili peppers. In greased 4 quart casserole, layer half of the noodles and half of the chicken. Season with salt and pepper. Top with half of the soup mixture and half of the cheese. Repeat layers. Bake, uncovered, 45 minutes.

"Ample and colorful - perfect for a family celebration, potluck or barbecue."

Alice Claiborne   **Fairfield High School, Fairfield, CA**

NOTES & REMINDERS

Barbecue Turkey Breast

Serves 4 - 6

16 ounces 7-Up
1 cup soy sauce
1 cup oil
$1/4$ teaspoon garlic powder
1 whole turkey breast OR 6 to 8 boneless chicken breasts

Combine first 4 ingredients for marinade. Bone and skin turkey breast. Slice into 4"
x 3 $1/2$" pieces. (Slightly frozen meat slices easier.) Marinate 24 hours. Barbecue over
low heat until done.

"I like to use chicken breasts instead of turkey because it's quicker to do."
Celeste Giron   **Riverton High School, Riverton, UT**

Grilled Turkey Loco with Cranberry Salsa

Serves 8 - 12

1 (12 pound) turkey
8 tablespoons butter (1 stick)
juice of 6 limes
2 tablespoons tequila
2 tablespoons fresh oregano, finely chopped
    OR 1 teaspoon dried oregano
salt and freshly ground pepper, to taste
2 cups fresh or frozen cranberries
4 teaspoons orange zest, grated
2 (large) oranges, peeled, membranes removed
$1/4$ cup onion, chopped
1 tablespoon fresh coriander, (cilantro) minced
1 tablespoon fresh ginger, minced
1 tablespoon jalapeño pepper, seeded

Ask your butcher to butterfly your turkey, cutting off excess skin and lumps of fat.
Wash and dry bird and insert a meat thermometer in the thickest part, not touching
the bone. Melt butter and add lime juice, tequila, oregano, salt and pepper. Place bird
skin side down on oiled grill, about 6" above heat. Mop bird with lime mixture. Grill
for about 15 minutes. Turn and mop again. Grill another 15 minutes. Turn and mop
with lime sauce every 20 minutes or so until thermometer registers 170 degrees,
about 1 $1/2$ to 2 hours. Meanwhile, prepare cranberry salsa: Chop cranberries coarsely
in food processor. Transfer to bowl and add orange zest. Coarsely chop oranges in
processor and add to cranberries with all remaining ingredients. Salt to taste. Mix
well and allow flavors to blend for at least 30 minutes. Serve at room temperature.

"A party favorite! Serve with fresh fruit, rellenos, etc."
Jeri Lundy   **Grossmont High School, La Mesa, CA**

NOTES & REMINDERS

85

Marinated Turkey Breast Fillets

Serves 4

  4 turkey breast fillets
  1 cup soy sauce
  1 cup 7-Up
  1 cup cooking oil

Combine soy sauce, 7-up and oil. Marinate fillets a minimum of 30 minutes and up to overnight. Use marinade to baste during grilling or microwave until partially done, then grill 5 to 8 minutes per side, until browned. Enjoy!

Joan Goodell   **Eldorado High School, Las Vegas, NV**

Jamaican Jerk Burgers

Serves 4

  1 teaspoon salt
  1 tablespoon pepper
  1 tablespoon thyme
  1 tablespoon + 1 teaspoon allspice
  1 Scotch bonnet (habanero) pepper, minced
  4 scallions, chopped
  1 pound ground turkey
  4 slices Muenster cheese
  1 onion, sliced
  1 tomato, sliced
  1 mango, peeled, sliced
  4 whole wheat buns

Mix together spices, Scotch bonnet pepper and scallions to make jerk seasoning. Use $1/4$ cup jerk seasoning and mix with 1 pound ground turkey. Store remaining seasoning for future use. Form into 4 patties. Barbecue until cooked through. Top burgers with a slice of cheese, onion, tomato and mango. Toast or grill buns.

Betty Plooy   **Vacaville High School, Vacaville, CA**

Main Dishes
BEEF • LAMB

Blue Cheese Stuffed Hamburgers
Serves 4

- 1 ¹/₂ pounds ground beef
- ¹/₂ teaspoon salt, divided
- ¹/₂ teaspoon pepper, divided
- ¹/₃ cup blue cheese, crumbled
- 3 ounces cream cheese, softened
- 1 tablespoon country-style Dijon mustard
- 4 onion buns
- 1 ¹/₄ cups fresh mushrooms, sliced
- 2 (medium) onions, sliced
- 1 tablespoons Worcestershire sauce
- 4 slices ripe tomato

Stir together ground beef, ¹/₄ teaspoon salt and ¹/₄ teaspoon pepper. Form into 8 large ¹/₄" thick patties. Stir together blue cheese, cream cheese and mustard. Place 2 tablespoons cheese mixture on top of each of 4 patties. Top each with remaining meat patty. Press around edges to seal. Cook in skillet over medium heat, turning once, until desired doneness (12 to 15 minutes for medium). Place hamburgers on buns. Cook mushrooms and onions in skillet with meat drippings, adding remaining ¹/₄ teaspoon salt, ¹/₄ teaspoon pepper and Worcestershire sauce. Place tomato slice on each hamburger and top with grilled mushrooms and onions.

Nan Paul   **Grant Middle School, Escondido, CA**

Wisconsin Cheese Stuffed Burgers
Serves 12   *Photo opposite page 65*

- 3 pounds ground beef
- ¹/₂ cup dry bread crumbs
- 2 eggs, beaten
- 1 ¹/₂ cups (5 ounces) your favorite Wisconsin cheese, shredded;
  OR Pepper Havarti cheese, shredded; OR blue cheese, crumbled;
  OR basil & tomato feta cheese, crumbled
- 12 hamburger buns

In a large mixing bowl, combine beef, bread crumbs and eggs; mix well but lightly. Divide mixture into 24 balls; flatten each on waxed paper to 4" across. Place 1 tablespoon cheese on each of 12 patties. Top with remaining patties, carefully pressing edges to seal. Grill patties 4" from coals, turning only once, 6 to 9 minutes on each side or until no longer pink. To keep cheese between patties as it melts, do not flatten burgers with spatula while grilling. Serve on hamburger buns. NOTE: Cheese filling may be very hot if eaten immediately after cooking.

Wisconsin Milk Marketing Board   **Madison, WI**

Sloppy Joes
Makes 8

2 pounds hamburger
1 onion, chopped
1 can tomato soup
$1/4$ cup catsup
1 tablespoon brown sugar
$3/4$ teaspoon chili powder
$3/4$ teaspoon Worcestershire sauce
$1/2$ teaspoon salt
$3/4$ teaspoon dry mustard
$1/4$ teaspoon curry powder
8 hamburger buns

Fry hamburger with onion; drain excess grease. Mix remaining in separate bowl and pour over cooked hamburger; stir to combine. Serve warm, spooned onto buns.

Camille Hicks   **Riverton High School, Riverton, UT**

Barbecue Sandwiches
Serves 8 - 10

1 (medium) onion, finely chopped
1 tablespoon olive oil
2 cups catsup
1 cup red wine vinegar
$1/2$ cup dark brown sugar, firmly packed
$1/4$ cup liquid smoke
$1/4$ cup Worcestershire sauce
3 cloves garlic, minced
2 jalapeño peppers, minced
2 teaspoons salt
1 teaspoon coriander seeds, crushed
1 teaspoon cumin seeds, crushed
1 (4 pound) beef brisket
8 to 10 (jumbo) hamburger buns

Cook onion in hot oil in medium saucepan until tender. Stir in catsup and next 4 ingredients. Combine garlic, jalapeño peppers, salt, coriander seeds and cumin seeds; stir well. Add to sauce mixture. Simmer, uncovered, over medium-low heat for 15 minutes. Trim excess fat from brisket. Place brisket on a sheet of heavy duty aluminum foil in a roasting pan. Spoon 1 cup sauce over brisket; seal foil around brisket. Bake at 325 degrees for 3 to 3 $1/2$ hours, or until meat is very tender. Let cool slightly; shred meat. Add 2 cups sauce to shredded meat. Serve on jumbo buns with remaining sauce.

"I serve this at parties and everyone loves them!"

Vicki Pearl   **Giano Intermediate School, La Puente, CA**

Barbecued Beef Sandwiches

Serves 6 - 8

1 medium onion, thinly sliced
$1/2$ cup beer
$3/4$ to 1 cup sweet barbecue sauce
$1/4$ cup brown sugar
$1/8$ cup molasses
$1/2$ to 1 pound tri-tip steak, trimmed of fat
salt and pepper, to taste
1 to 2 cups water
French rolls

Set crock pot to 325 degrees. Combine onion with beer, barbecue sauce, brown sugar and molasses. Add whole tri-tip, salt and pepper and 1 cup water. Let cook in crock pot 4 to 6 hours. Add remaining water as desired. If cooking on stove top, cook over low heat for 3 hours. Increase to medium heat for last 30 minutes to 1 hour. As tri-tip becomes tender, shred with a fork and continue cooking. Serve on sliced French rolls.

"This dish tastes best if cooked in a crock pot."

Marshawn Porter   **Arroyo Grande High School, Arroyo Grande, CA**

Carne Asada Tortas

Serves 4 - 6

1 1/2 pounds skirt steak
Marinade:
1/2 cup orange juice
2 teaspoons ground chili powder
1/2 teaspoon dried oregano
1/4 teaspoon ground cumin
1/2 (large) onion, sliced
1/2 (large) orange, sliced
1 lemon, sliced
1 lime, sliced
Chili Mayonnaise:
1/2 cup mayonnaise
1/2 teaspoon ground chili powder
1/4 teaspoon ground cumin
4 to 6 torta rolls (Mexican bollitos) or French rolls
vegetable cooking spray
Garnish: fresh salsa, sliced avocado, shredded lettuce

Place skirt steak in large ziploc bag. In a small bowl, whisk the orange juice, chili powder, oregano and cumin together; set aside. Place 1/2 of the onions and citrus fruits on each side of skirt steak in ziploc bag. Pour orange juice mixture over all. Close the bag and place in a container (in case it leaks) and refrigerate 2 to 4 hours, or overnight.

Chili Mayonnaise: In a small bowl, whisk mayonnaise, chili powder and cumin together. Cover and refrigerate until ready to use.

Preheat an outdoor grill to medium high. Slice torta rolls in half, lengthwise. Spray each side with vegetable cooking spray and place, cut side down, on heated grill. Cook 1 to 2 minutes, watching very carefully. Remove from gill and keep warm. Remove meat from marinade and grill 4 to 5 minutes per side, or until desired degree of doneness. Remove from grill to a rimmed cutting board and slice across grain of meat into 1/2" strips. Spread each half of torta roll with an equal portion of chili mayonnaise. Layer a portion of meat on bottom of each roll. Top with desired garnishes and serve.

"Try grilled boneless chicken breasts, adjust grilling time as necessary.
The carne asada is also great in burritos, quesadillas or just served on its own."
Karen Rogers Riedel   **Valhalla High School, El Cajon, CA**

Crockpot BBQ Beef

Serves 10

5 pounds roast beef
1 to 2 tablespoons oil
20 ounces catsup
1 onion, diced
1 teaspoon liquid smoke
1 cup brown sugar
$1/4$ cup cider vinegar
1 tablespoon mustard

Slice roast into thin slices; brown in skillet with small amount of oil. Transfer browned slices to crockpot and add remaining ingredients. Cook approximately 8 hours, or until roast shreds when stirred.

*"I got this recipe from my aunt in Iowa.
This recipe is easy, makes a lot and freezes well."*

Renee Paulsin **Hemet High School, Hemet, CA**

Foil Meal

Serves 4

4 hamburger patties
1 onion, sliced
4 potatoes, sliced
4 carrots, sliced
1 can cream of mushroom soup
salt and pepper, to taste

Tear 4 pieces of foil large enough to enclose hamburger patty and vegetables. Place a hamburger patty on each piece of foil; add slices of onion, potatoes and carrots. Top with 3 tablespoons mushroom soup. Season with salt and pepper. pull foil together, fold at top so juices won't run out. Bake at 375 degrees for 1 hour, 30 minutes. Serve immediately.

Laura Giauque **Olympus High School, Salt Lake City, UT**

NOTES & REMINDERS

Frito Delight

Serves 4

1 pound ground beef
1 (small) onion, chopped
1 can tomato sauce
1 can tomato paste
3 (tomato paste) cans water
2 tablespoons sugar
2 cloves garlic, minced
1 teaspoon chili powder
$1/2$ teaspoon cumin seed
1 teaspoon salt
1 cup rice, cooked
1 bag Fritos corn chips
Garnishes: Diced avocado, diced tomato, grated cheese,
    shredded lettuce, diced onion, salsa, sour cream

Brown ground beef and onion; drain excess grease. Stir in tomato sauce, tomato paste, water, sugar, garlic, chili powder, cumin seed and salt. Simmer, covered, 40 minutes. Add cooked rice. Serve on a bed or Fritos corn chips and top with condiments.

"Great for crowds. Set up in buffet style. Sauce mixture freezes well."
Brenda Umbro   **Orange Glen High School, Escondido, CA**

Quick Chili

Serves 4

3 (16 ounce) cans tomato sauce
1 envelope Chili-O seasoning mix
$1/4$ cup onion, chopped
1 pound ground beef, cooked, crumbled
1 (16 ounce) can beef and bean chili (optional)

Combine sauce, chili seasoning mix, onion, ground beef and chili, if using; simmer 15 to 20 minutes. Serve with choice of crackers.

Deloris Laughlin   **Western High School, Las Vegas, NV**

Tamale Loaf

Serves 6

1 tablespoon oil
2 cloves garlic, minced
2 (small) onions, chopped
1 pound hamburger
1 tablespoon chili powder
1 can creamed corn
1 (#10) can tomatoes
1 cup yellow corn meal
salt, to taste
2 eggs, beaten
1 can olives, pitted, drained
4 - 6 slices cheese

In oil, brown onion, garlic and hamburger; stir in chili powder. In saucepan over low heat, stir together creamed corn, tomatoes and cornmeal to make a mush. Add salt, 2 beaten eggs and olives. Combine with meat mixture and pour into greased baking pan. Top with cheese slices and bake at 350 degrees for 45 minutes or until casserole pulls away from sides.

Linda Melton Hayes   **Los Banos High School, Los Banos, CA**

Quick Tamale Pie Casserole

Serves 6 - 8

1 pound ground beef
2 cloves garlic, chopped
1 onion, chopped
4 to 6 XLNT tamales, coarsely chopped
1 cup frozen corn
1 to 2 (8 ounce) cans tomato sauce
1 teaspoon (or more) chili powder
salt and pepper, to taste
1 can black olives, sliced
1 cup cheddar cheese, shredded (optional)

Brown beef with garlic and onion; drain grease. Mix together with remaining ingredients, except cheese, and bake at 350 degrees in a 9" x 13" casserole dish for 45 minutes to 1 hour. Top with cheese, if desired, near end of baking time.

"I keep a supply of tamales in the freezer so this dinner can be prepared quickly."
Janet Riness   **Westminster High School, Westminster, CA**

NOTES & REMINDERS

93

Mexican Lasagna

Serves 8 - 10

2 pounds ground beef
$1/2$ cup onion, chopped
2 envelopes taco seasoning mix
$1 \, 1/3$ cups tomato sauce
$1 \, 1/3$ cups diced tomatoes, with liquid
nonstick cooking spray
4 (10") flour tortillas, cut into 2" strips
2 cups cheddar cheese, shredded, divided

In a heavy skillet over medium heat, brown ground beef and onion; drain off grease. Add taco seasoning mix, tomato sauce and tomatoes; bring to a boil. Reduce heat, cover and simmer 10 minutes. Spoon about 1 cup filling into a 9" x 13" x 2" glass baking pan, that has been sprayed with nonstick cooking spray. Top with a single layer of tortilla strips. Sprinkle with 1 cup cheese. Repeat layers one more time. Top with remaining meat sauce. Microwave on MEDIUM for 8 minutes. Top with remaining cheese. Microwave on HIGH 2 minutes more, or until cheese melts.

Linda Stroup　　　　　　　**Virgin Valley High School, Mesquite, NV**

Grandma's Old Country Swedish Meatballs

Serves 6 - 8

1 onion, chopped
2 to 4 tablespoons oil, divided
2 pounds hamburger
$1/2$ pound ground pork
3 raw potatoes, grated
2 eggs
pinch sage
$1/4$ teaspoon allspice
$1/4$ teaspoon nutmeg
$1/4$ teaspoon ground cloves
$1/2$ teaspoon salt
$1/8$ teaspoon pepper
2 slices bread
$1/2$ cup milk

Sauté onion in 1 tablespoon oil; remove and cool. Mix onion with hamburger, pork, potatoes, eggs and spices. In a small bowl, soak bread in milk; crumble and mix into hamburger-pork mixture. Shape mixture by rounded tablespoons into balls. In large skillet, heat 2 to 3 tablespoons oil. Slowly brown and cook meatballs. If desired, remove meatballs when done and make your favorite gravy.

"My grandmother brought this recipe from Finland as a teenager.
We have passed it through two generations in America. I pass it to you!"

AiliDee Karosich　　　　　　**Mira Mesa High School, San Diego, CA**

Swedish Meatballs Casserole

Serves 4

    1 pound ground beef
    1/4 pound seasoned ground pork (Jimmy Dean sausage in the roll)
    1 egg
    1/4 teaspoon nutmeg
    salt and pepper, to taste
    1 cup half & half
    1/2 cup cracker crumbs
    1 onion, thinly sliced
    1 can cream of mushroom soup

Mix together ground beef and pork, egg, seasonings, half and half and cracker crumbs. Roll into bite-sized balls or use a cookie scoop to form even size balls. Place meatballs on non-greased cookie sheet and bake at 350 degrees for 10 minutes. Turn or roll balls over and continue to bake for another 10 to 15 minutes, until evenly browned. Place meatballs in baking dish, cover with sliced onions and mushroom soup. Bake approximately 20 minutes, until sauce is bubbling. NOTE: Meatballs may be fried instead of baked. Recipe can be doubled or tripled easily.

"A family favorite and great at a buffet or a holiday meal with turkey or ham."
Barbara Allen   **Ayala High School, Chino Hills, CA**

Patty's Pepper Steak

Serves 6

    1/2 cup freshly cracked peppercorns
    3 pounds sirloin steak
    McCormick's Meat Marinade
    1/4 cup oil
    2 teaspoons vinegar
    1 tablespoon water
    1/4 cube butter
    3 tablespoons Worcestershire sauce
    3 tablespoons lemon juice

Crack peppercorns. Pound them into steak with a mallet. Marinate meat with McCormick's meat marinade, oil, vinegar and water for 4 hours. When ready to cook, drain marinade into saucepan and bring to a boil. Add butter, Worcestershire and lemon juice. Grill steak to your liking. Put on serving platter and cover with hot marinade. NOTE: If you pound the steaks thin, cooking time is less.

"This is a 20-year-old recipe. I have used it to dazzle friends at a barbecue cook out. Pat Mellenger, my sister-in-law, is the originator."
Sue Mellenger   **Dana Hills High School, Dana Point, CA**

NOTES & REMINDERS

Grilled Borracha Style Skirt Steak

Serves 6

Marinade:
$1/2$ cup beer
$1/4$ cup dry white wine
juice of 1 lime
1 teaspoon chili powder
$1/2$ teaspoon dried oregano
pinch cumin
2 $1/2$ to 3 pounds skirt steak
$1/2$ yellow onion, sliced
$1/2$ red onion, sliced
$1/2$ orange, sliced into rounds
1 lime, sliced into rounds
fresh cilantro sprigs
Garnish: Lime wedges; fresh cilantro sprigs; queso fresco
or farmer's cheese, crumbled

Marinade: Combine beer, wine, lime juice, chili powder, oregano and cumin in a non-aluminum mixing bowl; whisk until combined. Place the skirt steak in a large flat dish or heavy ziploc bag. Pour marinade over steak, then top with sliced onions, orange, lime and cilantro sprigs. Turn to coat well. Cover and marinate 2 to 4 hours. When ready to grill or broil, remove from marinade and grill 3 inches from heat, 4 to 6 minutes per side for medium rare. Cut into individual portions and garnish with lime wedges, fresh cilantro sprigs and crumbled cheese.

*"Try other cuts of steak, pork or even chicken.
The cooking time will need to be adjusted for each meat."*
Karen Rogers Riedel   **Valhalla High School, El Cajon, CA**

Rita & Gil's Famous Steaks

Serves 4

$1/4$ cup Worcestershire sauce
$1/4$ cup A-1 steak sauce
$1/4$ cup molasses
$1/4$ cup lime & lemon juice, combined
nonstick cooking spray
4 steaks, rib-eye, T-bone or filet mignon

Combine first four ingredients for marinade. Place steaks in a 9" x 13" pan that has been sprayed with nonstick cooking spray. Brush steaks, both sides, with marinade. Refrigerate 8 hours or overnight, covered with plastic wrap. When ready to serve, remove plastic wrap and replace with foil. Bake at 350 degrees for 15 to 20 minutes. Then, place on barbecue grill and grill 10 minutes on each side for well done.

"We created this watching the Cooking Channel and adding our own touches."
Rita Blohm   **Nogales High School, La Puente, CA**

Southwestern Kabobs

MAIN DISHES.....PAGE 105

Caribbean Teriyaki
Skewers

MAIN DISHES.....PAGE 78

Caribbean Lime Steak

Serves 4 - 6

$1/3$ cup lime juice (3 medium limes)
$1/4$ cup oil
$1/4$ cup molasses
2 tablespoons prepared mustard
1 teaspoon lime peel, grated
1 teaspoon garlic powder
$1/2$ teaspoon pepper
$1/2$ teaspoon salt
2 pounds flank steak
lime wedges

In a small bowl, mix lime juice, oil, molasses, mustard, lime peel, garlic powder, pepper and salt with a wire whisk. Score steak across top. Pour lime juice mixture over steak, turning to coat all sides. Refrigerate 4 to 8 hours or overnight, turning once or twice. Broil steak 3" from heat source, 3 minutes on each side for medium steak. Place on heated platter. Slice thinly on the diagonal. Serve garnished with lime wedges.

"Serve this with black beans, salsa fresca and tortillas. A true favorite at our house!"
Pam Ford   **Temecula Valley High School, Temecula, CA**

Barbecued Flank Steak

Serves 4 - 6

2 to 3 pounds flank steak
Adolf's Meat Tenderizer
$1/2$ cup Catalina salad dressing

Tenderize flank steak according to directions on Adolf's Meat tenderizer. In a 9" x 13" casserole dish, pour salad dressing on both sides of flank steak. Marinate approximately 10 to 30 minutes. Barbecue on both sides approximately 7 to 9 minutes per side. Slice thinly against the grain, at the diagonal. This may also be cooked under the broiler in the oven. NOTE: Scrape as much of the dressing as possible prior to cooking to avoid burning. Leftover marinade may be heated to boiling (to kill bacteria) and used for cut, cooked meat.

"This is always a crowd favorite!"
Liz Aschenbrenner   **Sierra High School, Manteca, CA**

NOTES & REMINDERS

Marinated Flank Steak

Serves 4

> 2 pounds beef flank steak
> 2 tablespoons garlic salt
> 2 tablespoons seasoned pepper
> $1/2$ cup Worcestershire sauce
> $1/4$ cup soy sauce
> $1/4$ cup olive oil
> $1/4$ cup lemon juice

Sprinkle flank steak with garlic salt and pepper. Place steak in a large, shallow roasting pan. In a small bowl, combine other ingredients for a marinade. Mix well, pour over steak. Cover pan and marinate in refrigerator 24 hours, turning several times. Remove from refrigerator 1 hour prior to cooking. Dry meat with paper towels. Reserve marinade and baste meat while cooking. Barbecue 4 minutes on each side for rare or longer for desired doneness.

"Our friends, Dolores and Glenn Gonzales-Hayes, prepared this for a church barbecue. It was absolutely delicious! I'm happy to pass their recipe on to you!"

Gaylen Roe   **Magnolia Junior High School, Chino, CA**

Marinated Tri-Tip

Serves 4

> $3/4$ cup soy sauce
> 2 cloves garlic, crushed
> 1 teaspoon ginger
> 1 tablespoon olive oil
> $1/2$ teaspoon coarse ground black pepper
> 1 $1/2$ pounds tri-tip steak

Combine soy sauce, garlic, ginger, oil and pepper in self sealing plastic bag; mix well. Add tri-tip and marinate 2 to 3 hours, turning several times. Grill tri-tip, uncovered, over indirect medium coals: 45 minutes for rare; 1 hour for medium rare. Turn occasionally.

Mary Oliveiro-Benito   **Central Valley High School, Redding, CA**

Teriyaki Marinated Strips
Serves 12

1 cup soy sauce
$3/4$ cup brown sugar
$1/4$ cup oil
2 tablespoons honey
2 tablespoons cooking sherry
4 cloves garlic, grated
$1/2$" piece fresh ginger, peeled, grated
1 tablespoon sesame seeds
4 green onions, thinly sliced
3 pounds London broil
bamboo skewers

Combine soy sauce with brown sugar, oil, honey, sherry, garlic, ginger, sesame seeds and onions. Remove fat from London broil and cut into $1/4$" strips. Marinate beef strips in marinade 5 hours. Soak bamboo skewers in water for one hour. Change the water one time. Place marinated meat on skewers and barbecue until desired doneness.

"Thanks to my sister-in-law and friend, Carole."
Jill Sweet Gregory   **Santa Paula High School, Santa Paula, CA**

Bul Kogi (Korean Barbecue)
Serves 4 - 6

3 to 4 pounds London broil, cut into 1" cubes
2 cloves garlic, crushed
$1/4$ cup sesame seeds, toasted, crushed
1 cup green onions, finely chopped
1 teaspoon pepper
1 teaspoon sesame oil
2 cups soy sauce
1 cup sugar
$1/4$ cup oil

Place beef cubes in large pan or dish. Stir in remaining ingredients and toss to coat meat well. Cover and let stand at room temperature 2 hours. Put cubes of meat on skewers. Barbecue over coals or under broiler, basting often with marinade until meat is cooked through.

"My father loved to barbecue and this was his favorite!
I make it often in his honor and my kids enjoy it as much as I did."
Peggy Goyak   **Birmingham High School, Van Nuys, CA**

NOTES & REMINDERS

Barbecued Beef Brisket

Serves 10

6 to 7 pound beef brisket
liquid smoke
salt
1 (large) onion, sliced
3 to 4 cloves garlic, chopped
Sauce:
3 tablespoons brown sugar
1 (small) bottle catsup
$^1/_2$ cup water
2 tablespoons liquid smoke
3 teaspoons dry mustard
2 teaspoons celery seed
6 tablespoons butter or margarine
salt and pepper, to taste

Rub liquid smoke and salt on both sides of brisket. Wrap in foil and refrigerate overnight. Next day, sprinkle onion and garlic on both sides of meat. Wrap tightly in heavy duty foil. Place in a large pan and bake at 300 degrees for 5 hours. Remove from oven and cool. Refrigerate overnight. *Prepare sauce:* Combine all sauce ingredients in saucepan and cook for 2 minutes. Pour over cooked meat. Bake at 350 degrees until hot, approximately 30 minutes. Slice and serve.

"I got this recipe from a friend from Texas. It is authentic and delicious. It takes 3 days, so plan ahead. It is well worth the effort. The sauce can be doubled."

Kathleen Dickerson   **Ruth O. Harris Middle School, Bloomington, CA**

Spicy Smoked Brisket & Barbecue Sauce
Serves 8

5 pounds beef brisket, trimmed
1 large clove garlic, minced
1 tablespoon liquid smoke
1 tablespoon chili powder
1 teaspoon paprika
1 teaspoon salt
$1/2$ teaspoon ground cumin
$1/2$ teaspoon sage
$1/2$ teaspoon sugar
$1/2$ teaspoon oregano
$1/4$ teaspoon cayenne pepper
$1/4$ teaspoon freshly ground pepper
Barbecue Sauce:
$1/2$ cup melted beef fat (from brisket)
$1 1/4$ cups catsup
$1/2$ cup Worcestershire sauce
$1/3$ cup fresh lemon juice
$1/4$ cup brown sugar, firmly packed
$1/4$ cup onion, chopped
$1/4$ cup water
1 tablespoon Tabasco sauce

Rub garlic on both sides of brisket. Spoon liquid smoke over both sides. Combine remaining spices in a small bowl, mixing well. Rub into brisket. Set brisket, fat side up, on a large pieces of foil; wrap tightly. Transfer to a shallow roasting pan. Bake at 200 degrees for about 8 hours, until tender. Remove from oven, reserving melted fat for barbecue sauce. Slice across the grain into thin slices and rewrap in foil to keep warm while preparing barbecue sauce. Pour fat from brisket into medium saucepan over low heat. Stir in remaining sauce ingredients and cook over low heat until thick, about 15 minutes. Serve with sliced brisket.

"The barbecue recipe that doesn't need a barbecue!"

Jill Marsh   **Warren High School, Downey, CA**

Char Broiled Brisket with Mopping Sauce

Serves 8

> 6 pounds beef brisket, flat cut, trimmed of fat
> 2 quarts water (approximate)
> 2 bay leaves
> 1 teaspoon pepper
> *Mopping Sauce:*
> 1 $^1/_2$ teaspoons dry mustard
> 1 teaspoon garlic powder
> $^1/_2$ teaspoon bay leaf, crumbled
> 1 teaspoon chili powder
> 1 $^1/_2$ teaspoons paprika
> 1 teaspoons Tabasco sauce
> $^2/_3$ cup Worcestershire sauce
> 2 $^2/_3$ cups meat stock from brisket

Place brisket into a large pot and cover $^3/_4$ of the way with water. Add bay leaves and pepper. Cover with lid and cook 3 to 4 hours on simmer, adding water if needed. Turn brisket every 30 minutes. When brisket is tender and done, drain off all liquid, reserving 2 $^2/_3$ cups for mopping sauce. Prepare mopping sauce by combining all sauce ingredients and mixing together. Place brisket on barbecue at medium heat. Brush with mopping sauce. Turn every 20 minutes and brush with sauce. Cook on grill 30 to 40 minutes. Place brisket on platter and slice into serving slices.

"The best barbecue brisket you will ever taste. It almost falls apart it is so deliciously tender. Warm the leftover sauce (in the microwave) and serve it on the side."

Marianne Traw   **Ball Junior High School, Anaheim, CA**

Apricot Curried Lamb (Sossaties)

Serves 6 - 8

> 2 large onions, chopped
> 1 clove garlic, crushed
> 2 tablespoons oil
> 2 cups stewed apricots, drained
> 1 to 1 $^1/_2$ cups water (depends on dryness of apricots)
> $^1/_4$ teaspoon cayenne pepper
> 1 tablespoon curry powder
> $^1/_2$ cup brown sugar
> $^1/_4$ cup apple cider vinegar
> $^1/_4$ teaspoon each salt and pepper
> 3 pounds lamb, cut into 1 $^1/_2$" cubes
> skewers

Brown onion and garlic in oil in a 3 quart saucepan. Add apricots and 1 cup water. Stir in cayenne, curry powder, brown sugar, vinegar, salt and pepper. Simmer mixture gently and cook 15 minutes. Add another $^1/_2$ cup water if too thick to use as marinade. Allow to cool. Pour marinade over cubed lamb. Let stand overnight in refrigerator. Skewer lamb and grill over medium/high heat until no longer pink in middle. Heat

---

NOTES & REMINDERS

sauce to a boil and brush over cooked meat.

"As an AFS student in South Africa in 1969-70, this was one of my favorite meals. It's great served with rice pilaf."

Linda Falkenstien   **Morro Bay High School, Morro Bay, CA**

Lamb Kabobs Indian Style
Serves 6 - 8

        4 to 6 cloves garlic,
        10 to 12 almonds
        1 teaspoon poppy seeds
        1 teaspoon garam masala
        $^1/_2$ teaspoon cayenne pepper
        2 cups plain yogurt
        2 pounds lamb, trimmed, cubed
        4 to 5 tablespoons ghee (clarified butter)
        2 bunches coriander leaves (cilantro)

Grind garlic, almonds, poppy seeds, garam masala, cayenne and yogurt to a paste. Marinate lamb cubes with this paste and refrigerate overnight. Put the lamb pieces on skewers and brush with melted ghee. Grill about 7 minutes each side over medium-low flame. Serve hot, garnished with chopped coriander leaves. NOTE: You can also bake the kabobs until well-browned and tender in a 400 degree oven.

"This is delicious with Indian bread and fried sliced onions."

Margo Olsen   **Amador Valley High School, Pleasanton, CA**

Wine & Rosemary Lamb Skewers
Makes 6

        1 cup dry red wine
        $^1/_4$ cup olive oil
        3 cloves garlic, slivered
        1 tablespoon fresh thyme, chopped (or 1 teaspoon dried thyme)
        1 tablespoon fresh rosemary, chopped
           (or 1 teaspoon dried rosemary, crumbled)
        2 pounds boneless lamb, cut into 1" cubes
        salt and pepper, to taste

Combine wine, oil, garlic, thyme and rosemary in a shallow glass dish. Add lamb cubes; cover and marinate in refrigerator up to 12 hours, turning several times. Remove lamb from marinade; discard. Thread lamb onto 6 long metal skewers. Season to taste with salt and pepper. Oil hot grill to help prevent sticking. Grill lamb on a covered grill over medium heat, 8 to 12 minutes, turning once or twice.

"Very tasty - you will enjoy every bite!"

Nancy Patten   **Placerita Junior High School, Newhall, CA**

NOTES & REMINDERS

Herb Topped Rack of Lamb

Serves 3

2 racks of lamb
$1/3$ cup Dijon mustard
1 cube butter
4 cloves garlic, minced
1 cup dry bread crumbs
3 tablespoons parsley, chopped

Heat grill. Brush lamb with mustard and grill 10 minutes on each side. Remove from grill. In a small pan, melt butter. Add minced garlic, bread crumbs and parsley. Brush remaining mustard on lamb; top with bread mixture and return to grill for 45 minutes. NOTE: I usually grill in a foil pan.

"My husband loves this lamb recipe.
If you like lamb, I think you will love this recipe!"

Linda Brayton   **Grace Davis High School, Modesto, CA**

Main Dishes
PORK

Marinated Pork Chops
Serves 6

$1/2$ cup orange juice
$1/4$ cup soy sauce
$1/2$ cup apricot jam
2 tablespoons lemon juice
6 (1" thick) pork chops

Combine first four ingredients. Marinate pork chops in sauce for 1 hour. If desired, brush sauce on pork chops before grilling. Grill on medium heat 5 to 8 minutes per side.

Melanie Haderlie   **Granger High School, West Valley City, UT**

Party Pork Chops
Serves 12

12 pork chops, thick cut
$1/2$ teaspoon salt
$1/2$ cup catsup
3 tablespoons brown sugar
$1/4$ cup vinegar
1 (9 ounce) can crushed pineapple
1 tablespoon soy sauce

Place pork chops in a 9" x 13" baking pan. Combine remaining ingredients to make sauce; pour over pork chops. Bake, uncovered, at 300 degrees for 2 hours.

Diana Lee   **David A. Brown Middle School, Wildomar, CA**

Southwestern Kabobs
Serves 4   *Photo opposite page 96*

4 boneless top loin pork chops, cut into 1" cubes
4 tablespoons taco or fajita seasoning
$1/2$ green, red and/or yellow bell pepper, seeded and cut into 1" pieces
$1/2$ (large) onion, peeled, cut into 1" pieces
4 green onions, cut into 2" pieces, leaving tops on

In a plastic bag or shallow bowl, toss together pork cubes with desired seasoning until pork is evenly coated. Thread pork cubes, alternating with pepper, onion and green onion pieces, onto skewers. Grill over a medium-hot fire, turning occasionally, until pork is nicely browned.

National Pork Producers Council   **Des Moines, IA**

Oven Barbecue Country Ribs

Serves 8 - 10

> 10 to 12 country-style pork spare ribs
> 1 jar chili sauce
> 12 ounces brandy
> 1 cup brown sugar, firmly packed

Place the ribs in a spacious roasting pan. Mix the chili sauce, brandy and brown sugar thoroughly. Pour over ribs and bake slowly, covered, at 325 degrees for 3 hours.

"This goes great with herb broccoli-rice and Caesar salad."

Gail McAuley   **Lincoln High School, Stockton, CA**

Oven Barbecued Spare Ribs

Makes 4 - 6

> 4 to 5 pounds pork spare ribs
> 1 to 2 teaspoons salt and pepper
> 1 lemon, thinly sliced
> 1 (large) onion, finely chopped
> 1 teaspoon celery salt
> 1 teaspoon chili powder
> $1/4$ cup brown sugar
> $1/4$ cup vinegar
> $1/4$ cup Worcestershire sauce
> 1 cup tomato catsup
> 2 cups water

Cut ribs into pieces 3 to 4 ribs wide. Place meaty side up in a shallow baking dish. Salt and pepper. Place a thin slice of lemon on each piece. Sprinkle with onion. Place in a 450 degree oven, uncovered, for 45 minutes to brown. Meanwhile, mix remaining ingredients together and bring to a boil. Pour the sauce over the ribs after they are browned and reduce heat to 350 degrees. Roast 1 to 1 $1/2$ hours in uncovered pan. Baste and turn ribs occasionally.

"Chicken may be substituted for the pork."

Bonnie Shrock   **Kearny High School, San Diego, CA**

Best Ever Baby Back Ribs

Serves 4

> 4 pounds pork baby back ribs
> 3 cloves garlic, minced
> 1 tablespoon sugar
> 1 tablespoon paprika
> 2 teaspoons salt
> 2 teaspoons chili powder
> 2 teaspoons ground cumin
> *Barbecue Sauce:*
> 1 (small) onion, finely chopped
> 2 tablespoons butter or margarine
> 1 cup catsup
> $1/4$ cup brown sugar, firmly packed
> 3 tablespoons lemon juice
> 3 tablespoons Worcestershire sauce
> 2 tablespoons vinegar
> 1 $1/2$ teaspoons ground mustard
> 1 teaspoon celery seed
> $1/8$ teaspoon cayenne pepper

Rub ribs with garlic; place in a shallow roasting pan. Cover and bake at 300 degrees for 2 hours; cool slightly. Combine sugar, paprika, salt, chili powder and ground cumin; rub over ribs. Cover and refrigerate 8 hours or overnight. In a saucepan, sauté onion in butter until tender. Stir in remaining sauce ingredients; bring to a boil. Reduce heat; cook and stir until thickened, about 10 minutes. Remove from heat; set aside $3/4$ cup. Brush ribs with some of the remaining sauce. Grill, covered, over medium heat for 12 minutes, turning and basting with sauce. Serve with reserved sauce.

Anita Cornwall   **Cimarron-Memorial High School, Las Vegas, NV**

Tomato Cream & Sausage Sauce Fettucini

Serves 6

> 2 tablespoons olive oil
> 3 shallots, chopped
> 4 cloves garlic, chopped
> 1 pound sweet Italian sausages, casings removed
> 1 cup whipping cream
> 2 (14.5 ounce) cans diced tomatoes, in juice, with Italian seasoning
> 1 $1/2$ tablespoons dried sage
> $1/2$ teaspoon dried crushed red pepper
> $3/4$ pound fettucini
> salt and pepper, to taste
> $1/2$ cup Parmesan cheese, grated

Heat oil in heavy large pot over medium-high heat. Add shallots and garlic and sauté until softened, about 3 minutes. Add sausage and sauté until no longer pink, breaking

NOTES & REMINDERS

107

up with back of fork, about 5 minutes. Add whipping cream; simmer 5 minutes. Stir in tomatoes, with juice, sage and crushed red pepper. Simmer until sauce thickens, stirring occasionally, about 15 minutes. Meanwhile, cook pasta in large pot of boiling salted water until al dente. Drain pasta, reserving $1/2$ cup cooking liquid. Return pasta to pot, add sauce and toss over medium heat until sauce coats pasta, adding reserved cooking liquid by $1/4$ cupfuls if mixture is dry. Season with salt and pepper. Transfer to bowl, sprinkle with Parmesan and serve.

"This is a great one dish meal to bring to a potluck."

Jamey Davis   **Redwood Middle School, Thousand Oaks, CA**

BBQ Chinese Pork

Serves 4 - 6

    6 cloves garlic, finely minced
    2 tablespoons ginger, minced
    2 teaspoons salt
    2 tablespoons soy sauce
    3 tablespoons honey
    I cup sherry
    I cup stock
    I teaspoon 5-Spice powder
    2 pound pork tenderloin or roast

Place all marinade ingredients in a saucepan and heat just until simmering; simmer 2 to 3 minutes. Cool marinade until cold. In a Ziploc bag, place pork and marinade. Allow to marinate in refrigerator 24 hours. When ready to cook, remove from marinade and cook over a hot, indirect grill or fire until well done. Brush marinade over meat often to coat. Cut into thin slices to serve.

"This is excellent hot or cold, served with plum, hoisin and mustard sauces."

Priscilla Burns   **Pleasant Valley High School, Chico, CA**

Pork Satay with Peanut Sauce

Serves 4

Marinade:
$1/4$ cup peanut oil
$1/2$ teaspoon ground ginger
$1/2$ teaspoon ground cumin
2 teaspoon ground coriander
1 (medium) onion, sliced
$1/8$ teaspoon ground pepper
2 tablespoons lemon juice, freshly squeezed, OR sherry
3 tablespoons light brown sugar
2 tablespoons soy sauce
1 $1/4$ pounds boneless lean pork loin, trimmed of fat,
    cut into 12 $1/2$" thick slices
12 (8" to 10") wooden skewers,
    soaked in cold water for 30 minutes, drained
Hot Peanut Sauce:
1 $1/2$ cups chicken broth
3 cloves garlic, minced
1 (small) onion, minced
$3/4$ cup chunky peanut butter
3 tablespoons light brown sugar
$1/2$ teaspoon red pepper flakes
1 tablespoon cilantro, chopped
Garnishes: $1/3$ cup cilantro, chopped; 1 lime, sliced

Combine marinade ingredients and pour into a large ziploc bag. Add meat slices and seal bag. Place in a shallow dish and marinate, refrigerated, for 2 to 4 hours, turning bag once. Meanwhile, *prepare sauce:* Heat broth in a medium saucepan. Add garlic, onion and peanut butter. Mix in brown sugar, red pepper flakes and cilantro; simmer 3 minutes; set aside. Prepare grill; oil grate. Remove meat from marinade and thread the strips tightly onto skewers. When coals are ashen, set the skewers perpendicular to the oiled grate (or use an oiled grill screen). Grill 1 $1/2$ to 2 minutes on each side or until pork is cooked through. Serve hot, sprinkle with cilantro and garnish with lime slices. Pass the peanut sauce separately. NOTE: Flank steak may be substitited for pork.

"This recipe may sound unusual, but it is absolutely delicious! Satay is from Indone-sian cuisine. The pepper flakes can be adjusted for more or less heat."
Patti Bartholomew   **Casa Roble High School, Orangevale, CA**

NOTES & REMINDERS

BBQ Pork Tenderloin with Red Currant Sauce

Serves 6

3 to 4 pounds pork tenderloin
Marinade:
$1/2$ cup sherry
$1/2$ cup soy sauce
2 cloves garlic, minced
2 tablespoons dry mustard
1 teaspoon thyme
1 teaspoon ground ginger
Red Currant Sauce:
1 (10 ounce) jar red currant jelly
2 tablespoons sherry
1 tablespoon soy sauce
$1/4$ cup dried currants

Place pork tenderloin in ziploc bag. Mix marinade ingredients together and pour over pork; seal bag. Marinate pork 4 to 8 hours, refrigerated. Barbecue or roast according to time recommended for size of tenderloin. Cook until golden brown on all sides, turning often, if grilling. Meanwhile, make sauce. Mix jelly with sherry and soy sauce in pan. Add currants and cook 2 to 5 minutes over medium-low heat. Let cool to thicken. Pour sauce over cooked, sliced pork and enjoy!

"I was given this recipe by a close friend who is a fabulous cook. It is great served with grilled asparagus, roasted red potatoes and a tossed salad."

Sue Campbell   **Marsh Junior High School, Chico, CA**

Grilled Lime-Marinated Pork Tenderloin

Serves 4 - 5

1 $1/2$ pounds pork tenderloin
juice of 2 limes, about 3 tablespoons
4 tablespoons vegetable oil
2 teaspoons ground cumin
1 teaspoon dried oregano
2 cloves garlic, crushed
1 fresh jalapeño chile, chopped
$1/2$ teaspoon pepper, freshly ground
$1/2$ teaspoon salt

Place pork in shallow nonmetallic dish or heavy plastic bag. Combine remaining ingredients and pour over pork tenderloin. Turn the meat in the marinade to coat thoroughly and refrigerate for at least 6 hours. Preheat grill to medium and sear the meat on both sides. Cook about 30 minutes at medium to low heat, basting with marinade and turning every 5 to 10 minutes to cook evenly.

Cheryl Clubb   **Saddleback High School, Santa Ana, CA**

Barbecue Pork Sandwiches

Serves 8 - 10

    4 to 5 pounds pork tenderloin
    $\frac{1}{2}$ cup butter or margarine
    I jar chili sauce
    $\frac{1}{2}$ cup vinegar
    I cup brown sugar
    I teaspoon onion powder
    I teaspoon garlic powder
    salt and pepper, to taste
    2 to 3 cups cole slaw, prepared
    8 to 10 Vienna or sweet French rolls, sliced in half

Barbecue pork over medium coals approximately 3 hours, until internal temperature reaches 170 degrees. Meanwhile, melt margarine or butter over low heat in medium saucepan. Add chili sauce, vinegar, brown sugar, onion and garlic powder, and salt and pepper. Heat slowly. After pork has been cooking 2 hours, baste with barbecue sauce every 10 to 15 minutes for last hour of cooking. Remove and cool slightly. Slice into $\frac{1}{4}$" thick slices. Place sliced meat, a scoop of cole slaw and extra sauce on rolls and serve.

"A traditional family recipe, always a winner. Meat can be barbecued in advance, sliced and put into extra barbecue sauce. For serving, reheat in microwave."
Debra Truitt   **Woodland High School, Woodland, CA**

Grilled Pepperoni Pizza

Serves 4

    I pre-made pizza crust, such as Boboli
    I cup pizza sauce
    8 ounces mozzarella cheese, shredded
    Toppings: Sliced pepperoni, sliced mushrooms,
        bell pepper strips, sliced onion

Heat grill. Assemble pizza by spreading sauce on crust and topping with cheese and desired toppings. Place pizza directly on grill and grill until cheese is melted and bubbly.

"This is a great way to have pizza during the summer without heating up the house!"
Debbie Harvey   **Amador Valley High School, Pleasanton, CA**

NOTES & REMINDERS

111

Main Dishes
SEAFOOD

Barbecued Stuffed Shrimp
Serves 6

2 tablespoons butter
2 tablespoons onion, chopped
2 tablespoons celery, chopped
2 tablespoons green pepper, chopped
2 tablespoons flour
$1/2$ cup milk
$1/4$ cup bread crumbs
I cup crab meat, cooked
I $1/2$ teaspoons Worcestershire sauce
$1/2$ teaspoon parsley, chopped
$1/4$ teaspoon salt
$1/4$ teaspoon pepper
3 dozen large shrimp
I cup barbecue sauce

Melt butter in skillet; sauté onion, celery and green pepper over medium heat. Stir in flour and milk, stirring constantly until thick. Add bread crumbs, crab meat, Worcestershire sauce, parsley, salt and pepper; mix well. Shell and de-vein shrimp, leaving on tails. Slit back of shrimp. Put two shrimp together with crab stuffing. Hold together with toothpicks. Chill until ready to cook. Broil 5 inches from heat. Baste occasionally with your favorite barbecue sauce until shrimp are done, about 5 minutes on each side.

"Gourmet group loved this recipe! Impressive to serve.
Easy to prepare ahead and cook when guests arrive."

Janis Brokaw   **Mountain Shadows Middle School, Rohnert Park, CA**

Bryan's Marinated Salmon
Serves 2 - 4

> 1 can whole cranberries
> $3/4$ cup cranberry juice
> $1/4$ cup soy sauce
> 1 tablespoon garlic, minced
> 1 tablespoon brown sugar
> 1 $1/2$ teaspoons ginger, grated
> 1 teaspoon sesame oil
> 2 to 4 salmon fillets

Place all ingredients in a gallon sized ziploc bag; marinate 1 $1/2$ to 2 hours. Remove salmon and pat dry. Fry in skillet with small amount oil or grill on barbecue. Remove salmon from heat and keep warm once it browns. Put marinade ingredients in skillet and reduce, about 5 minutes. Pour thickened marinade as a sauce over salmon and serve.

"This recipe was worked out by my son-in-law, Bryan. His wife, the non-cook, raves about it, as do I."

Sue Walters   **Morse High School, San Diego, CA**

Dilly Salmon Fillets
Serves 4

> 4 (5 to 6 ounce) fresh or frozen salmon fillets, $1/2$" thick
> 3 tablespoons lemon juice
> 2 tablespoons fresh dill, snipped, divided
> 2 tablespoons mayonnaise
> 2 teaspoons Dijon mustard
> dash pepper

Rinse fish fillets and pat dry with paper towels. Place in a shallow dish. In a small bowl, combine lemon juice and 1 tablespoon dill; pour over fish, turning to coat. Cover and marinate 10 minutes. In another small bowl, stir together remaining dill, mayonnaise, mustard and pepper; set aside. Drain fish. Place fish on greased grill rack. Cover and grill about 3 minutes. Turn fish, spread with mayonnaise mixture. cover and grill 2 to 6 minutes more, until fish flakes easily when tested. NOTE: Halibut steaks may be substituted for the salmon.

"Here's a dazzling salmon recipe that's as easy as tossing fish on the grill!"

Sharron Maurice   **Blythe Middle School, Blythe, CA**

NOTES & REMINDERS

Grilled Salmon Fillets, Asparagus & Onions

Serves 6

$1/2$ teaspoon paprika, preferably sweet Hungarian
6 salmon fillets, 6 to 8 ounces each
$1/3$ cup bottled honey-Dijon marinade OR barbecue sauce
1 bunch (about 1 pound) fresh asparagus spears, ends trimmed
1 (large) red or sweet onion, cut into $1/4$" slices
1 tablespoon olive oil
salt and pepper, to taste

Prepare grill. Sprinkle paprika evenly over salmon fillets. Brush marinade or barbecue sauce over salmon; let stand at room temperature 15 minutes. Brush asparagus and onion slices with olive oil; season with salt and pepper. Place salmon, skin side down, in center of grill over medium coals. Arrange asparagus spears and onion slices around salmon on grill. Grill salmon and vegetables over covered grill 5 minutes. Turn asparagus and onion slices. Grill 5 to 6 minutes more or until salmon flakes easily when tested with a fork and vegetables are crisp-tender. Separate onion slices into rings; arrange over asparagus.

"Great flavor, simple and nice presentation.
By grilling the vegetables along with the salmon, it's quick."
Colleen Easton   **Brea Olinda High School, Brea, CA**

Salmon Steaks

Serves 4

4 salmon steaks, approximately $1/2$ pound each, $3/4$" thick
salt and pepper, to taste
$1/4$ cup bottled Italian dressing or hickory flavored dressing
$1/2$ teaspoon paprika
1 teaspoon onion, minced or grated
2 teaspoons lemon juice

Sprinkle both sides of salmon steaks with salt and pepper. Combine salad dressing, paprika, onion and lemon juice. Pour over steaks. Make sure both sides are coated. Let stand 20 minutes. Lift steaks from marinade, reserving marinade. Place on heavy duty foil and turn up edges to form a shallow pan. Place pan on barbecue grill 4 to 6" above bed of coals. Make a hood of foil to enclose fish if cooking on an open grill. Cook, basting frequently with marinade, for approximately 20 minutes or until salmon flakes at the thickest portion.

"Garnish with fresh parsley!"
Kathie Baczynski   **Mt. Carmel High School, Poway, CA**

Salmon Barbecue

Serves 3 - 4

> $1/2$ cup real maple syrup
>   1 tablespoon soy sauce
>   3 to 4 salmon steaks or fillets

Combine syrup and soy sauce. Marinate fillets at least 30 minutes in mixture or overnight. Grill or broil until fish is done.

"Use real maple syrup!"

Nancy Eckhout   **Brighton High School, Salt Lake City, UT**

Salmon Steaks on the BBQ

Serves 6

>   2 cups catsup
>   4 cloves garlic, minced
>   2 tablespoons parsley, chopped
> $1/2$ cup soy sauce
>   1 (large) onion, sliced
>   1 (large) lemon, thinly sliced
>   2 - 4 pounds salmon steaks

Mix together catsup, garlic, parsley and soy sauce. Place a large sheet of foil on counter. Arrange sliced onions and lemons the length of salmon. Place salmon on top of onions and lemons. Pour sauce on top of salmon. Fold foil to close. Place on barbecue and cook until salmon flakes easily, about 20 to 30 minutes.

"Delicious served with pineapple."

Jan Tuttle   **Mills High School, Millbrae, CA**

Chili-Rubbed Alaska Halibut Kabobs

Serves 8

>   juice of 1 to 2 limes
>   3 cloves garlic, divided
>   1 jalapeño pepper, seeded, diced
> $1/2$ red onion, diced
> $1/2$ avocado, peeled, diced
>   1 (large) tomato, diced
>   2 tablespoons fresh cilantro, minced
>   salt and pepper, to taste
>   1 tablespoon chili powder
>   4 tablespoons fat free Italian salad dressing
>   2 pounds Alaska halibut, thawed, cut into 1" cubes
>   8 skewers

Combine half the lime juice, 1 clove minced garlic, jalapeño pepper and onion to a mixing bowl. Add the avocado, tomato and cilantro; toss gently, trying not to mash the avocado. Taste, add more lime juice, as necessary; salt and pepper to taste. Set salsa aside in refrigerator. Mix the chili powder with salad dressing; stir in 2 cloves lightly crushed garlic. Toss and lightly rub the halibut cubes with the chili mixture and let marinate, refrigerated, for 1 to 2 hours. Place 5 to 6 cubes halibut on each of the 8 skewers, turning until juices run clear, approximately 8 to 15 minutes, depending on the thickness of the fish. Place on serving platter and serve with salsa.

Terry Kluever   **Coronado High School, Henderson, NV**

Grilled Swordfish with Cilantro Butter

Serves 4

4 (8 ounce) center-cut, fresh swordfish fillets
2 tablespoons olive oil
1 bunch cilantro
$1/_2$ cup unsalted butter
juice of 1 lemon
salt and freshly ground pepper, to taste

Prepare charcoal. Lightly coat fillets with olive oil. When coals are ready, place fish on oiled grill and cook until just firm to the touch, about 4 minutes per side for thick fillets, less for thinner fillets; don't overcook. Wash cilantro thoroughly and remove thick stems. Combine cilantro with butter in food processor or blender with metal blade and mix for several seconds until light and fluffy. Blend in lemon juice. Season with salt and pepper. Serve fish with cilantro butter. NOTE: Swordfish is especially good cooked over mesquite charcoal.

"Cilantro butter is also delicious with seafood such as salmon or shrimp on bread."
Holly Gaddis   **El Capitan High School, Lakeside, CA**

Main Dishes

Roasted Vegetable Sandwich
Serves 4

   1 eggplant, peeled
   2 (medium) zucchini
   1 onion
   1 pound whole mushrooms
   2 tablespoons olive oil
   garlic salt, to taste
   black pepper, to taste
   wooden or metal skewers
   4 French rolls
   8 slices Provolone cheese
   1 jar roasted red peppers

Slice eggplant, zucchini and onion into thin slices. Wash and dry mushrooms. Coat all fresh vegetables with olive oil, using a pastry brush. Season with garlic salt and pepper. Skewer fresh vegetables and barbecue or broil until tender - don't let them burn! In the meantime, slice French rolls in half and melt 1 slice cheese on each side. Top with roasted red peppers. Remove roasted vegetables from skewers and layer on top of peppers. Serve warm. NOTE: Soak wooden skewers in water for 5 minutes before using to prevent them from burning on the barbecue.

"This is a great sandwich for all seasons and one of my all time favorites!"
Alicia Pucci   **Kenilworth Junior High School, Petaluma, CA**

Aunt Clementine's Eggplant-Zucchini Casserole
Serves 12

   1 ripe eggplant
   3 to 4 zucchini
   1 (15 ounce) can tomato sauce
   2 tablespoons oil
   1 teaspoon oregano
   garlic powder, to taste
   salt and pepper, to taste
   1 to 2 onions, sliced
   2 fresh tomatoes, sliced
   1 pound jack cheese, sliced

Slice eggplant and zucchini; place in colander, cover and set aside. In saucepan, combine tomato sauce with oil, oregano, garlic powder, salt and pepper. Simmer 10

117

minutes. Spread small amount of sauce in a 9" x 13" baking dish. *Layer as follows:* eggplant, zucchini, onion slices, tomato slices, cheese slices, sauce. Repeat, ending with sauce. Bake at 350 degrees for 1 hour or until vegetables are tender.

"This is for a crowd that appreciates fresh ingredients and healthy food."
Diane Lizardi   **Downey High School, Downey, CA**

Macaroni and Cheese for Adults

Serves 8

12 ounces bacon
5 (large) cloves garlic
1 cup heavy cream
1 cup half & half
1 (large) egg
$1/2$ teaspoon nutmeg, freshly grated
2 cups cheddar cheese, shredded, divided
2 cups Fontina cheese, shredded, divided
1 $1/2$ cups Parmesan cheese, freshly grated
12 ounces tube, elbow or other macaroni, cooked, drained
2 cups bread crumbs
1 to 2 tablespoons butter

Chop bacon and cook until crisp; drain, reserving 1 tablespoon drippings. Cook garlic in drippings about 1 minute; set bacon and garlic aside. Whisk cream, half & half, egg and nutmeg in heavy saucepan to blend. Add 1 $1/2$ cups cheddar cheese, 1 $1/2$ cups Fontina cheese and all of the Parmesan cheese. Stir over medium heat until cheeses are melted. Pour sauce over cooked pasta, stirring to coat. Stir in bacon and garlic. Season to taste with salt and pepper. Pour into buttered casserole dish or 9" x 13" pan. Sprinkle with remaining cheeses. Melt butter and toss with bread crumbs. Sprinkle crumbs over pasta. Bake in preheated 425 degree oven until sauce bubbles and crumbs are browned, about 30 minutes. NOTE: I often make this ahead and refrigerate, then bake just before serving. Add 15 to 20 minutes to cooking time. Panko (Japanese-style) or seasoned Italian bread crumbs can be substituted for bread crumbs. Leftover ham works well in place of bacon.

"Favorite casserole to take to my husband's family reunion every year.
It is also a great comfort food and good enough to share with company."
Laura de la Motte   **Turlock High School, Turlock, CA**

Macaroni & Cheese Deane

Serves 6

> 4 cups elbow macaroni
> 2 tablespoons butter or margarine
> $1/3$ cup milk
> $1/2$ can mushroom soup
> $1/2$ pint sour cream
> $1/2$ pint cottage cheese
> $1/2$ pound cheddar cheese, shredded, divided
> $1/3$ cup (or more) garlic croutons

Cook macaroni in boiling water until tender; drain. Stir in butter until melted. Add milk, soup, sour cream, cottage cheese and $3/4$ of the shredded cheese. Mix well and turn into a 9" x 13" casserole dish. Top with remaining cheese and croutons. Bake at 350 degrees for 45 minutes.

"I always double this recipe and put one in the freezer for another quick dinner."
Beverly Ranger   **Carpinteria High School, Carpinteria, CA**

Grilled Italian Vegetables with Pasta

Serves 6

> 1 (1 $1/4$ pound) eggplant, cut into $1/2$" thick slices
> 1 teaspoon salt, divided
> $3/4$ cup zucchini, quartered, lengthwise
> 1 red bell pepper, seeded, quartered
> nonstick cooking spray
> 4 plum tomatoes, halved
> 4 cups (2 bunches) green onions, sliced into 3" slices
> 2 tablespoons extra-virgin olive oil
> 1 tablespoon lemon rind, grated
> $1/2$ cup fresh basil, thinly sliced
> 6 cups penne, hot, cooked (about 12 ounces)
> $1/4$ cup fresh Parmesan cheese, grated

Place eggplant in colander, sprinkle with $3/4$ teaspoon salt. Toss gently to coat. Cover and let stand 30 minutes. Rinse eggplant with cold water and drain well. Prepare grill. Place eggplant, zucchini and bell pepper on grill rack coated with nonstick cooking spray. Grill 10 minutes, turning once. Add tomatoes and onions; cook 5 minutes, turning often. Remove vegetables from grill, cut all into 1" pieces, except tomato. Cut tomato halves lengthwise. Combine $1/4$ teaspoon salt, oil, lemon rind and basil in large bowl. Add vegetable mixture, pasta and cheese. Toss well.

"Salting the eggplant pulls out some of the bitter flavor. Grilled vegetables taste great on their own. Toss vegetables with little olive oil before grilling."
Sue Hope   **Lompoc High School, Lompoc, CA**

NOTES & REMINDERS

Spinach & Asiago Cheese Frittata
Serves 12

1 leek, thinly sliced
2 cloves garlic, minced
2 tablespoons olive oil
4 cups fresh spinach, torn
1 yellow or red bell pepper, roasted, cut into thin strips
$3/4$ cup Asiago cheese, shredded, divided
1 $1/2$ teaspoons fresh thyme, snipped
   OR $1/4$ teaspoon dried thyme, crushed
$1/4$ teaspoon salt
$1/8$ teaspoon pepper
6 eggs, slightly beaten

Cook leek and garlic in hot oil in a 10" ovenproof skillet over medium heat about 2 minutes or until tender, stirring frequently. Add spinach; cook and stir about 1 minute more until spinach is limp. Remove from heat. Stir in pepper strips, $1/2$ cup Asiago cheese, thyme, salt and pepper. Add eggs, stirring to mix well. Bake at 350 degrees for 13 to 15 minutes or until a knife inserted near center comes out clean. Loosen edges and bottom of frittata, if necessary, with a knife or spatula. Transfer to a serving plate. Sprinkle remaining Asiago cheese over top of frittata and cut into wedges.

"Both young and old like this one!"

Peggy Herndon   **Central Valley High School, Shasta Lake City, CA**

Desserts

French Chocolate Cake & Fudge Frosting

Serves 8 - 12

Cake:
$^1/_2$ cup butter
3 squares unsweetened chocolate
1 cup water
2 cups sugar
2 cups flour
2 eggs
1 teaspoon vanilla
$^1/_2$ cup sour milk
1 teaspoon soda
$^1/_4$ teaspoon salt

Frosting:
$^1/_2$ cup butter
2 squares unsweetened chocolate
6 tablespoons milk
1 (1 pound) box powdered sugar
1 teaspoon vanilla
1 cup walnuts, chopped

Cake: Bring butter, chocolate and water to a boil; remove from heat and stir in sugar and flour. Beat in eggs, vanilla, sour milk, soda and salt. Bake in a 9" x 13" pan or (2) 8" or 9" layers for 25 minutes at 325 degrees. Remove from oven and cool completely. Remove from pan(s) after 10 minutes.

Frosting: Bring butter, chocolate and milk to a rolling boil. Remove from heat and beat in powdered sugar, vanilla and nuts. Frost cooled cake.

"I probably make this recipe more often than any other.
It's great when you need a chocolate fix."

Kathy Warren   **C.K. McClatchy High School, Sacramento, CA**

Grandma Jo's Chocolate Fudge Cake

Serves 12

Cake:

2 cups flour
2 cups sugar
2 teaspoons baking soda
$1/2$ cup butter or margarine
1 cup sour cream
2 eggs
6 tablespoons unsweetened cocoa
1 teaspoon vanilla
$1/2$ cup boiling water

Frosting:

$1/2$ cup butter
3 tablespoons unsweetened cocoa
6 tablespoons milk
1 (1 pound) box powdered sugar

Prepare cake: In a large mixing bowl, combine and mix together the flour, sugar, baking soda, butter and sour cream. Add eggs, cocoa and vanilla and beat. Beat in boiling water. Grease and flour (2) 9" round cake pans. Line the bottoms with waxed paper and grease paper. Pour batter into prepared pans and bake at 350 degrees for 25 to 30 minutes. Meanwhile, *prepare frosting:* In a large saucepan, combine butter, cocoa and milk; bring to a boil, remove from heat and stir in powdered sugar, stirring until smooth. Cool. Frost cooled cake.

> *"My most requested recipe. For the chocoholic!*
> *Sprinkle the top of the cake with chopped nuts or chocolate shots."*

Beth Guerrero   **Selma High School, Selma, CA**

Chocolate Fudge Bundt Cake

Serves 16

1 chocolate fudge cake mix (Duncan Hines without pudding)
1 (3.9 ounce) package instant chocolate pudding
4 eggs
1 (8 ounce) carton sour cream
$1/2$ cup strong coffee
$1/2$ cup oil
1 (12 ounce) package semi-sweet chocolate chips

Preheat oven to 350 degrees. Mix all ingredients except chocolate chips in a large bowl and beat with electric mixer for 5 minutes. Stir in chocolate chips and mix well. Pour into a greased bundt pan and bake 1 hour. Remove from oven and cool. Unmold onto serving dish and serve.

> *"This easy to make dessert is always a big hit.*
> *Serve it with whipped cream and fresh strawberries. It stays moist for several days."*

Jan Neufeld   **Fullerton High School, Fullerton, CA**

NOTES & REMINDERS

122

Pig Pickin' Cake (Fresh Fruit Cake)
Serves 12

1 package yellow cake mix
³/₄ cup Crisco oil
4 eggs
1 (11 ounce) can mandarin oranges, drained
1 (large) can crushed pineapple, slightly drained
9 ounces Cool Whip
1 (3 ounce) package instant vanilla pudding
Garnish: Fresh kiwi, strawberries, oranges, pineapple, etc.

Combine cake mix with oil, eggs and oranges using an electric mixer; place in (4) 9"
round cake pans. Bake at 350 degrees for 15 minutes, or until done. Cool and remove
from pans. Mix pineapple with vanilla pudding and blend well. Fold in Cool Whip. Ice
layers. Garnish with desired fresh fruit.

"This is a beautiful cake!"

Diane Cluff   **Provo High School, Provo, UT**

Ruby Slipper Cake
Serves 10 - 12

1 package yellow cake mix
1 cup sour cream
³/₄ cup sugar
2 eggs
1 (3 ounce) package raspberry Jello
1 (8 ounce) container raspberry yogurt
1 (small) container Cool Whip

Combine first 4 ingredients in a large mixing bowl; blend 2 minutes. Prepare a
microwave safe bundt cake pan by lightly coating inside with butter and dusting with
granulated sugar. Spoon ¹/₃ of batter into bundt pan. Sprinkle half of the jello over
the batter. Repeat layers. Microwave 6 minutes + 45 seconds on SIMMER or LEVEL 3,
then 4 minutes + 30 seconds on HIGH. Allow cake to stand 5 minutes before removing
from pan. Cover with plastic wrap until cool. Combine yogurt with Cool Whip and
frost cooled cake. NOTE: For microwaves less than 900/1000 watts: Cook 9 minutes on
SIMMER and 6 minutes on HIGH.

*"This is a very attractive cake and always impresses my students when
I use it as a demonstration recipe."*

Janet Policy   **Ramona High School, Riverside, CA**

NOTES & REMINDERS

123

Party Rum Cake
Serves 10

1 cup pecans or walnuts, chopped
Cake:
1 (18.5 ounce) package yellow cake mix
1 (1.75 ounce) package instant vanilla pudding
4 eggs
$^1/_2$ cup cold water
$^1/_2$ cup oil
$^1/_2$ cup Bacardi dark rum (80 proof)
Glaze:
$^1/_4$ cup butter
$^1/_4$ cup water
1 cup granulated sugar
$^1/_2$ cup Bacardi dark rum (80 proof)

Preheat oven to 325 degrees. Grease and flour 10" tube or 12 cup bundt pan. Sprinkle nuts over bottom of pan. Mix all cake ingredients together. Pour batter over nuts. Bake 1 hour. Cool. Invert onto serving plate. Prick top. *For glaze:* Melt butter in saucepan. Stir in water and sugar. Boil 5 minutes, stirring constantly. Remove from heat, stir in rum. Spoon and brush glaze evenly over top and sides. Allow cake to absorb glaze. Repeat until all glaze is used up. NOTE: If using yellow cake mix with pudding already in the mix, omit instant pudding mix; use 3 eggs instead of 4; $^1/_3$ cup oil instead of $^1/_2$ cup oil.

"This recipe was given to me by my son, Vincent. It's one of his personal favorites."
Darlene Brown   **Golden Valley Middle School, San Bernardino, CA**

Lil's Cherry Pudding Cake
Serves 8

Cake:
$^1/_2$ cup shortening
2 $^1/_2$ cups sugar, divided
2 eggs
2 $^1/_2$ cups flour
1 $^1/_2$ teaspoons baking powder
$^1/_2$ teaspoon soda
$^1/_2$ teaspoon salt
1 cup milk
2 cans cherries, drained
Glaze:
dash salt
4 tablespoons cornstarch
1 $^1/_2$ cups cherry juice
$^1/_2$ cup water
$^1/_2$ teaspoon almond flavoring

Cream shortening and 1 $^1/_2$ cups sugar. Add eggs and beat well. Sift together flour, baking powder, soda and salt. Add alternately to creamed mixture with milk. Mix well. Stir in cherries. Pour into greased 8" x 10" glass pan and bake at 350 degrees for 45 minutes. While baking, combine remaining 1 cup sugar with dash salt, cornstarch, cherry juice, water and almond flavoring. When cake has cooled slightly, drizzle with cherry sauce. Serve warm.

"One of mom's favorites to bring to family gatherings."
Sonja Tyree   **Ayala High School, Chino Hills, CA**

Pudding Cake
Serves 12

$1/_2$ cup cocoa
1 cup brown sugar
2 cups hot water
$1/_2$ (16 ounce) package miniature marshmallows
1 white cake mix, prepared batter
1 cup walnuts, chopped (optional)
Whipped cream

Mix the first 3 ingredients in an 11" x 14" pan. Put miniature marshmallows on top of mixture. Pour prepared cake batter on top of marshmallows and add nuts, if using. Bake at 350 degrees for 40 to 45 minutes, or until cake is done. Serve warm with whipped cream.

"So yummy - yet so easy to prepare!"
Kathy Rudelich   **Hillcrest High School, Midvale, UT**

Lemon Cake
Serves 18 - 20

Cake:
1 lemon cake mix
1 (small) package lemon jello
4 eggs
$1/_2$ teaspoon lemon extract
$3/_4$ cup oil
$3/_4$ cup water
Glaze:
$1 1/_2$ cups powdered sugar
$1/_2$ cup lemon juice

Beat all cake ingredients together on low for 30 seconds. Beat on medium speed for 2 minutes. Pour into a 9" x 13" greased and floured pan. Bake at 350 degrees for 30 to 35 minutes. Remove from oven and poke holes in cake with a fork. Mix together powdered sugar and lemon juice. Pour over cake. Cool before serving.

"If you like lemon, you will love this simple cake!"
Cindy Bowman   **McFarland High School, McFarland, CA**

NOTES & REMINDERS

Lori's Favorite Frosting

Serves 2 cups

> 1 tablespoon meringue powder
> 3/4 cup sugar
> 1/2 cup water
> 1 cup margarine
> 1 cup shortening
> 2 teaspoons vanilla
> 2 pounds powdered sugar

Beat together meringue powder, sugar and water until stiff peaks form. In separate bowl, mix together margarine, shortening and vanilla. Slowly beat in powdered sugar. Add meringue to mixture and beat about 5 minutes, until light and fluffy.

"This is the best recipe for frosting and also decorating!
I have used it in making cakes for family and also lovely wedding cakes."
Lori Konschak **Ceres High School, Ceres, CA**

Chocolate Cherry Cake

Serves 12

> 2 eggs, slightly beaten
> 1/2 teaspoon vanilla
> 1 can Comstock ruby red cherry pie filling
> 1 package devils food cake mix
> 1 cup sugar
> 1/3 cup milk
> 5 tablespoons butter
> 1 cup chocolate chips

Slightly beat eggs and add vanilla. Mix cake mix with cherry filling; using a wooden spoon stir in eggs and vanilla in thirds. Pour into greased 9" x 13" pan and bake at 350 degrees for 40 to 45 minutes. Meanwhile, in a saucepan, stir together sugar, milk and butter; bring to a boil for 1 minute. Remove from heat. Stir in chocolate chips. Cool slightly and spread over cooled cake.

"Delicious moist cake! Great with vanilla ice cream or whipped cream."
Adriana Molinaro **Granite Hills High School, El Cajon, CA**

Cherry Dump Cake

Serves 12 - 15

> 2 cans cherry pie filling
> 1 box white cake mix
> 1/4 cup margarine

Spray a 9" x 13" pan with nonstick cooking spray. Pour pie filling into pan. Sprinkle dry cake mix over cherries. Cut margarine into pieces and place evenly over cake mix. Cook at 350 degrees for 45 minutes. NOTE: You can vary the flavor by changing the pie filling to blueberry or apple, etc..

126

*"Since high school I've made this a thousand times!
It's very popular at potlucks and in my daughter, Andrea's college dorm!"*
Gaylen Roe   **Magnolia Junior High School, Chino, CA**

Apple Cobbler Cake
Serves 8

6 to 8 (large) green apples, peeled, sliced
2 $^3/_4$ cups sugar, divided
2 teaspoons cinnamon
$^1/_2$ cup butter or margarine, softened
4 eggs
2 cups flour

Place peeled and sliced apples into a 13" x 9" baking pan. In a small bowl mix $^3/_4$ cup sugar and cinnamon. Sprinkle apples with half of the sugar/cinnamon mixture. In separate bowl, cream butter and 2 cups sugar. Add eggs and flour. Mix well and pour over apples. Spread to cover. Sprinkle remaining cinnamon/sugar mixture over top. Bake at 325 degrees for 60 to 70 minutes. Serve hot or cold.

"This is a hit as a dessert or for a brunch. Try it a la mode!"
Karen Lopez   **San Luis Obispo High School, San Luis Obispo, CA**

NOTES & REMINDERS

Quick & Easy Peach Cobbler
Serves 16 - 20

2 boxes pre-made pie crust
2 teaspoons sugar
6 teaspoons cinnamon, divided
1 (6 pound) can peaches in heavy syrup
2 cups brown sugar
$^1/_2$ cup Karo syrup
2 teaspoons cloves
1 stick butter or margarine
2 tablespoons cornstarch
2 tablespoons vanilla

Preheat oven to 375 degrees. In a 9" x 13" casserole dish, place enough pie crust to cover bottom of pan. Sprinkle with 2 teaspoons sugar and 1 teaspoon cinnamon; prick with fork. Place in oven and bake until lightly browned, about 10 minutes. While crust is baking, combine all remaining ingredients in a large Dutch oven, including peach syrup, and simmer over medium heat for 10 to 15 minutes. Fill pie crust with filling, place remaining crust on top. With a fork, prick pastry to prevent puffing. Bake at 375 degrees for 30 to 45 minutes or until golden brown. NOTE: To protect from spills, place pan on baking sheet or place a sheet of foil on bottom of oven.

*"Serve this scrumptious cobbler warm and top with vanilla ice cream.
It's sure to be a hit, and they'll ask you to bring it every time!"*
Donna Baker   **Redlands East Valley High School, Redlands, CA**

Oatmeal Apple Crumble

Serves 6

4 cups apples, peeled, cored, sliced
$1/2$ cup applesauce
nonstick cooking spray
$1/2$ cup brown sugar, packed
$1/2$ cup flour
$3/4$ cup oats
$3/4$ teaspoon ground cinnamon
$3/4$ teaspoon ground nutmeg
$1/2$ cup margarine, cut into small pieces

Preheat oven to 350 degrees. Mix cut apples and applesauce together. Place in an 8"
square pan, that has been sprayed with nonstick cooking spray. Blend brown sugar
with flour, oats, spices and margarine until crumbly. Spread over apples. Bake 30 to
35 minutes until topping is golden brown. Allow to cool. Serve, topped with whipped
cream or ice cream.

"This dessert smells great as it's cooking!"

Marleigh Williams   **Corning High School, Corning, CA**

Chocolate Chip Peanut Butter Squares

Makes 12 bars   *Photo opposite*

1 $1/2$ cups powdered sugar
1 $1/2$ cups creamy peanut butter
1 $1/2$ teaspoons vanilla
1 (18 ounce) package Pillsbury Refrigerated Chocolate Chip Cookies

Heat oven to 350 degrees. In a medium bowl, combine powdered sugar, peanut butter
and vanilla; mix well. Remove cookie dough from wrapper. With floured fingers, press
half of dough in bottom of ungreased 8 or 9" square pan. Press peanut butter mixture
evenly over dough. Crumble and sprinkle remaining half of cookie dough over peanut
butter mixture. Carefully spread as evenly as possible. Bake at 350 degrees for 30 to
35 minutes or until golden brown and firm to the touch. Cool 30 minutes. Refrigerate
1 hour or until chilled. Cut into bars. Serve chilled or at room temperature.

Pillsbury Company   **Minneapolis, MN**

Chocolate-Chip Peanut
Butter Squares
DESSERTS.....PAGE 128

Cherry Berry
Ricotta Shortcake
DESSERTS.....PAGE 139

Chocolate Punch Bowl Cake

Serves 15

- 1 chocolate cake mix, prepared according to package directions
- 2 (large) packages Jell-O Chocolate Pudding,
  prepared according to package directions
- 1 package Skor candy pieces
- 2 cups walnuts, chopped
- 16 ounces Cool Whip

Prepare cake and chocolate pudding, according to directions on each package; allow to cool. Mix together candy pieces and walnuts, set aside. In a large punch bowl, break half of the cake into pieces. Top with half of the chocolate pudding. Cover with half of the Cool Whip and sprinkle with half of the candy/nut mixture. Repeat. Serve immediately.

> *"This is a great recipe that looks appealing in a punch bowl.
> The toffee pieces are a sweet surprise that makes this dessert one of my favorites."*

Jennifer Lufkin   **Valencia High School, Placentia, CA**

Key Lime Bars

Makes 20 bars

- 1 cup coconut, shredded, divided
- $3/4$ cup unsalted butter, cold, cut into 12 pieces
- $1/2$ cup powdered sugar
- 1 $1/2$ cups all-purpose flour
- 3 eggs + 2 yolks
- $1/2$ teaspoon salt
- $1/3$ cup Key lime juice
- zest of 3 limes, minced
- 1 $1/2$ cups sugar

Preheat oven to 325 degrees. Toast all of the coconut by spreading on cookie sheet and placing in oven 5 minutes, or until it begins to turn light brown. Line a 9" x 13" pan with parchment paper that has been lightly buttered on both sides. In bowl of a food processor fitted with metal blade, place cold butter, sugar, flour and $1/2$ cup toasted coconut. Process until ingredients resemble a coarse meal. Press mixture into prepared pan. Bake in preheated oven 15 minutes. Meanwhile, prepare filling by mixing eggs, yolks, salt, Key lime juice, zest and sugar until thoroughly blended. Pour filling over baked crust. Return to oven and bake 25 minutes. Halfway through baking time, top with remaining $1/2$ cup toasted coconut and turn pan to ensure even browning. Bars will be firm when done. Cool and cut into squares.

Marion S. Anderson   **A. G. Currie Middle School, Tustin, CA**

NOTES & REMINDERS

129

California Brownies

Makes 48 bars

Brownies:
2 cups flour
2 cups granulated sugar
$1/_2$ cup butter or margarine
$1/_2$ cup shortening
1 cup water
$1/_4$ cup unsweetened cocoa
$1/_2$ cup buttermilk
2 eggs, or 4 egg whites
1 teaspoon baking soda
1 teaspoon vanilla
Frosting:
$1/_2$ cup butter or margarine
2 tablespoons unsweetened cocoa
$1/_4$ cup milk
3 $1/_2$ cups powdered sugar
1 teaspoon vanilla

Prepare brownies: Combine flour and sugar; set aside. In heavy saucepan, combine butter, shortening, water and cocoa. Stir and heat to boiling. Pour boiling mixture over flour and sugar in bowl. Add buttermilk, eggs, baking soda and vanilla; mix well, using high speed on mixer. Pour into a well greased 17 $1/_2$" x 11 $1/_2$" jelly roll pan. Bake at 400 degrees for 20 minutes. *Prepare frosting* while brownies bake: In a saucepan, combine butter, cocoa and milk. Heat to boiling, stirring constantly. Mix in powdered sugar and vanilla until smooth. Pour warm frosting over brownies as soon as you remove them from the oven. Cool and enjoy.

> *"This is a favorite potluck recipe for Boy Scout Awards dinner.*
> *They disappear quickly. I also take these to family reunions."*

Judie Huffman   **Mariposa Co. High School, Mariposa, CA**

Fudge Nut Brownies

Serves 12 - 15

1 (12 ounce) package chocolate chips, divided
$1/_4$ cup margarine or butter
2 cups baking mix (such as Bisquick)
1 (14 ounce) can sweetened condensed milk
1 egg
1 teaspoon vanilla
1 to 1 $1/_2$ cups walnuts, chopped

Preheat oven to 350 degrees. In large saucepan over low heat, melt 1 cup chocolate chips with margarine or butter; remove from heat. Add baking mix, milk, egg and vanilla. Stir in nuts and remaining 1 cup chocolate chips. Pour into a well greased 13" x 9" baking pan. Bake 20 to 25 minutes or until brownies begin to pull away from sides of pan. Cool and cut into bars.

"This is my favorite brownie recipe. It is very easy, even for beginning cooks!"
Jeanette Atkinson   **Brinley Middle School, Las Vegas, NV**

Jan's Famous Caramel Brownies

Serves 8 - 12

I box German chocolate cake mix
I stick butter, melted
I (small) can evaporated milk, divided
$^1/_2$ cup walnuts, chopped
I bag semi-sweet or milk chocolate chips
I (large) bag caramels

Preheat oven to 350 degrees. Stir together cake mix with butter, $^1/_4$ cup evaporated milk and walnuts. Press half of the dough into a well greased 9" x 12" pan. Push dough up sides slightly. Bake 6 minutes. In microwave, melt caramels with approximately $^1/_8$ cup evaporated milk, stirring every 30 seconds until melted. Use enough milk to produce a smooth consistency for pouring. Remove crust from oven (it will still look doughy) and pour the chocolate chips evenly over top of crust. Pour melted caramels on top and crumble remaining dough over all. Return to oven and bake 15 minutes more. Cool completely. Cut into bars.

"Rich and chewy but oh so good! A hit at every barbecue."
Jeanette Neese   **Enterprise High School, Redding, CA**

Mint Brownies

Serves

I package brownie mix, prepared
Filling:
2 cups powdered sugar
2 tablespoons milk
$^1/_2$ cup butter, melted
$^1/_2$ teaspoon peppermint extract
2 drops green food coloring
Topping:
6 ounces chocolate chips
5 to 6 tablespoons butter (not margarine)

Prepare brownies according to package directions. Spread on an ungreased jelly roll pan and bake at 350 degrees for 20 to 25 minutes. Cool, then freeze dough 10 to 15 minutes. Mix together filling ingredients. Spread on cooled, frozen brownies. Freeze 10 to 15 minutes, until filling is hardened. In microwave, melt chocolate chips with butter, stirring every 30 seconds until smooth. Spread on top of frozen brownies. Refrigerate until topping has hardened. Cut into 2" squares. Serve.

"Always a hit. You can make different flavors by substituting the flavoring and color in the filling. My family loves lemon brownies and cinnamon brownies!"
Mary Nafis   **Montclair High School, Montclair, CA**

Praline Brownies

Makes 12

1 package of your favorite brownie mix
$1/2$ pound brown sugar, firmly packed
1 cup walnuts or pecans, chopped
2 tablespoons butter, melted

Prepare brownie mix according to package directions. Spread into a 9" x 13" pan. In a bowl, mix together brown sugar, nuts and butter. Sprinkle mixture over brownie mix. Bake at 350 degrees for 25 to 30 minutes.

"I have been making these for years. They're always a hit!"
Rebecca Harshbarger   **Chaparral High School, Temecula, CA**

Peanut Butter Picnic Bars

Serves 6 - 8

1 cup sugar
1 cup corn syrup
dash salt
2 cups peanut butter
4 cups crisp rice cereal
Topping:
$1/2$ cup butter or margarine
$1/2$ cup brown sugar
2 tablespoons milk
1 teaspoon vanilla
2 $1/2$ cups powdered sugar

Stir sugar, corn syrup and salt over medium heat until sugar is dissolved. Stir in peanut butter until smooth. Stir in cereal and coat completely. Press into cookie sheet or 9" x 13" pan. *Topping:* Bring butter and brown sugar to a boil. Add milk, vanilla and powdered sugar. Mix well with spoon or beater. Spread on bars while still warm.

Camille Hicks   **Riverton High School, Riverton, UT**

Peanut Chews

Serves 10 - 12

Crust:
1 package Pillsbury Moist Supreme yellow cake mix
$1/3$ cup margarine or butter, softened
1 egg
Topping:
3 cups miniature marshmallows
$2/3$ cup corn syrup
$1/4$ cup margarine or butter
2 teaspoons vanilla
1 (10 ounce) package peanut butter chips
2 cups crisp rice cereal
2 cups salted peanuts

Heat oven to 350 degrees. In large bowl, combine cake mix, $1/3$ cup margarine and egg at low speed until crumbly. Press into bottom of ungreased 9" x 13" pan. Bake 12 to 18 minutes or until lightly golden brown. Remove from pan and immediately sprinkle with marshmallows. Return to oven and bake an additional 1 to 2 minutes, or until marshmallows just begin to puff; cool. Meanwhile, in large saucepan, combine corn syrup, $1/4$ cup margarine, vanilla and peanut butter chips; heat just until chips are melted and mixture is smooth, stirring constantly. Remove from heat; stir in cereal and peanuts. Immediately spoon warm topping over marshmallows and spread to cover. Refrigerate until firm. Cut into bars. Store in covered container.

*"My Advance Foods class discovered this recipe and loved it.
Many are making Peanut Chews at home for all of their friends."*

Myrna Westmoreland   **Grace Davis High School, Modesto, CA**

Magic Marshmallow Puffs

Makes 16

$1/4$ cup sugar
2 tablespoons flour
1 teaspoon cinnamon
2 (8 ounce) cans refrigerated crescent dinner rolls
16 large marshmallows
$1/4$ cup margarine, melted
$1/2$ cup powdered sugar
$1/2$ teaspoon vanilla
2 to 3 teaspoons milk

Preheat oven to 375 degrees. In a small bowl, combine sugar, flour and cinnamon. Separate dough into 16 triangles. Dip 1 marshmallow in margarine; roll in sugar mixture. Place marshmallow on wide end of triangle. Roll up, starting at wide end of triangle and rolling to opposite point. Completely cover marshmallow with dough; firmly pinch edges to seal. Dip one end in remaining margarine; place margarine side down in ungreased large muffin cup. Repeat with remaining marshmallows. Bake 12 to 15 minutes, or until golden brown. Remove from muffin cups immediately; cool on wire racks. In small bowl, blend powdered sugar, vanilla and enough milk for desired drizzling consistency. Drizzle over warm rolls.

"Food student, Krystle Miller, showed this recipe in class, it's become a favorite!"

Sue Ogden   **San Clemente High School, San Clemente, CA**

Chocolate Mini Cheesecakes

Serves 12

Crust:
3/4 cup vanilla wafers, crushed
3 tablespoons butter, melted
3 tablespoons powdered sugar
3 tablespoons cocoa

Filling:
1/4 cup cocoa
2 tablespoons butter, melted
12 ounces cream cheese, softened
1/2 can sweetened condensed milk
1 1/2 eggs
1 teaspoon vanilla

Glaze:
1 cup semi-sweet chocolate chips
1/2 cup whipping cream
1/2 teaspoon vanilla

Heat oven to 300 degrees. Paper line 12 muffin cups. *Prepare crust:* Stir together crushed vanilla wafers, melted butter, powdered sugar and cocoa. Press 1 heaping tablespoonful of crust onto bottom of each cup. *Prepare filling:* Stir together cocoa and butter. Beat cream cheese until fluffy; beat in cocoa mixture. Gradually beat in sweetened condensed milk. Beat in eggs and vanilla. Spoon mixture into muffin cups and bake 35 minutes or until set. Cool. *Prepare glaze:* Melt chocolate chips with whipping cream and vanilla. Stir until smooth; immediately pour over cooled filling.

Barbara Stetler   **Ponderosa High School, Shingle Springs, CA**

Mom's Monster Cookies

Makes 30 - 35

2 1/2 cups brown sugar
1 1/2 cups white sugar
4 sticks margarine, softened
4 eggs
1/2 teaspoon Molly McButter seasoning
1 teaspoon baking soda
1 teaspoon baking powder
3/4 teaspoon salt
2 teaspoons vanilla
3/4 cup wheat germ
5 cups oatmeal
4 cups flour
2 (12 ounce) bags chocolate chips

Cream together first 3 ingredients for 5 to 10 minutes, until light and fluffy. Add eggs, Molly McButter, baking soda, baking powder, salt, and vanilla; mix well. In separate bowl, combine wheat germ with oatmeal and flour. Slowly add to creamed mixture. Stir in chocolate chips. Refrigerate 3 to 4 hours or overnight. Roll into balls and bake at 350 degrees for 10 to 15 minutes, until light brown.

"These cookies are very popular among friends, family and anyone else who has tried them."

Jill Enright   **Cerro Villa Middle School, Villa Park, CA**

Surprise Fudge Cupcakes

Serves 24

1 chocolate fudge cake mix, prepared
8 ounces cream cheese
1 egg
1/3 cup sugar
1 cup semisweet chocolate chips

Prepare cake mix according to package directions; pour into 24 lined cup cake pans, 2/3 full. Mix together cream cheese, egg and sugar until smooth. Stir in chocolate chips. Top each cup cake with a tablespoon of cream cheese mixture. Bake at 350 degrees 25 to 30 minutes, until center springs back when pressed with finger.

"Simple to make. Easy to take to special events."

Diedre Goodnough   **Norwalk High School, Norwalk, CA**

Ice Cream Cone Cakes

Makes 6 - 7 cakes

> 1 (10.7 ounce) package cake mix, any flavor
> 6 to 7 flat bottomed ice cream cones
> 1 can ready made frosting, any flavor
> cake decorations

Put oven rack in middle of oven. Preheat to 350 degrees. Prepare cake mix as directed on package. Using a muffin pan, place ice cream cones in muffin holes. Fill each cone to within $\frac{1}{4}$" of top. Bake 30 minutes or until top springs back. Cool, frost and decorate. Enjoy the smiles!

"Popular on-the-go treats for children. Now that I'm a Nana, Taylor and Austin have reminded me with their smiles and 'more please Nana!'"

Shirley Blough   **Hillside Middle School, Simi Valley, CA**

Pecan Tarts

Makes 18 - 24

> 6 ounces cream cheese, softened
> 1/ 2 pound + 3 tablespoons butter, divided, at room temperature
> 2 cups flour
> 3 eggs, well beaten
> 2 cups light brown sugar
> 1 teaspoon vanilla
> dash salt
> 1 cup pecans, chopped

Mix together cream cheese, $\frac{1}{2}$ pound butter and flour with a pastry blender. Flour your fingers and form dough into balls about the size of large marbles. Press balls into muffin pan cups so that dough covers bottom and comes halfway up the sides of each cup. Melt remaining 3 tablespoons butter and allow to cool. Combine cooled butter with eggs, brown sugar, vanilla and dash of salt. Fill crusts with filling halfway full. Sprinkle tops of each cup with 1 teaspoon chopped pecans. Bake at 350 degrees for 15 to 20 minutes.

"A family favorite. Great to make during the holidays to put on a cookie tray."

Susan Lefler   **Ramona Junior High School, Chino, CA**

Fruit Pizza

Serves 8 - 12

> 1 package refrigerated sugar cookie dough
> 1 (8 ounce) package cream cheese, softened
> $\frac{1}{4}$ cup sugar
> $\frac{1}{2}$ teaspoon vanilla
> fresh fruits, sliced, such as strawberries, kiwi, bananas, grapes
> 1 jar apple jelly, melted OR strawberry glaze

Preheat oven to 350 degrees. Slice cookie dough into $\frac{1}{4}$" thick slices and place on

NOTES & REMINDERS

round pizza pan. Press together to form a crust and bake 15 minutes or until golden brown; cool. Mix together cream cheese, sugar and vanilla. Spread onto cooled crust. Decorate with sliced fruits. Lightly brush on melted apple jelly or strawberry glaze, covering fruit. Serve immediately or refrigerate until ready to serve.

"We make this in class and the students all go home and make them for their families. They are great to take to potlucks or parties."

Libby Newman   **West Valley High School, Hemet, CA**

Strawberry Pie

Serves 6

    2 baskets fresh strawberries
    1 9" pie shell, baked
    1 cup sugar
    3 tablespoons cornstarch
    juice of 1 lemon (2 tablespoons)
    1 cup water
    red food coloring
    Whipped cream (optional)

Hull, wash and drain fruit. Place dry fruit in pie shell with pointed ends facing up. In medium sized saucepan, mix sugar with cornstarch. Slowly add water, lemon juice and red food coloring; mix well. Cook over medium heat until thickened, stirring occasionally to prevent sticking. Slowly spoon over fruit, covering each strawberry. Cool. Serve with whipped cream, if desired.

"Quick to make and the presentation is terrific!"

Maridel Anagnos   **Tokay High School, Lodi, CA**

Strawberry Cream Pie

Serves 6

    1 prepared crust, baked
    2 $1/2$ cups strawberries, divided
    1 (12 ounce) package cream cheese
    $1/4$ cup sugar
    $1/2$ teaspoon vanilla
    dash nutmeg
    1 cup whipping cream
    $1/4$ cup powdered sugar

Bake pie crust. Mash 1 cup strawberries; slice 1 cup strawberries and set aside. Leave $1/2$ cup strawberries whole, for garnish. Mix cream cheese, sugar, vanilla and nutmeg with electric mixer. Blend mashed strawberries into cream cheese mixture. In another bowl, whip whipping cream, adding powdered sugar gradually as you mix. Fold whipped cream into cream cheese mixture. Fold remaining 1 cup sliced strawberries into filling. Spoon into baked crust. Chill several hours before serving. Garnish with whole strawberries, if desired.

Carol Kagy   **Norwalk High School, Norwalk, CA**

NOTES & REMINDERS

137

Caramel Pecan Cheesecake

Serves 12 - 16

> 1 $\frac{1}{2}$ cups all purpose flour, divided
> 2 cups granulated sugar, divided
> $\frac{1}{4}$ cup + 1 tablespoon butter or margarine, divided
> 1 egg yolk
> 3 tablespoons + 1 $\frac{1}{2}$ cups whipping cream, divided
> 4 (8 ounce) package cream cheese, softened
> 1 cup light brown sugar, firmly packed
> 1 tablespoon vanilla, divided
> $\frac{1}{4}$ teaspoon salt
> 4 (large) eggs
> 1 cup pecan halves, toasted

In a food processor, process 1 $\frac{1}{4}$ cups flour with $\frac{1}{2}$ cup sugar and butter or margarine for 30 seconds. Add egg yolk and 3 tablespoons whipping cream; process until crumbly. Press firmly into a 9" springform pan. Bake at 400 degrees for 15 minutes or until browned. Cool on wire rack. Using an electric mixer, beat $\frac{1}{2}$ cup sugar with cream cheese and brown sugar in large mixing bowl at medium speed until fluffy. Add remaining $\frac{1}{4}$ cup flour and beat at low speed until blended. Add $\frac{1}{2}$ cup whipping cream, 2 teaspoons vanilla and salt, beating well. Add eggs, one at a time, beating just until blended. Pour over cooled crust. Bake at 325 degrees for 1 hour or until set. Turn off oven and cool cheesecake in oven with oven door partially open for 1 hour. Cover and chill overnight. Melt remaining $\frac{1}{2}$ cup sugar in a heavy saucepan over medium-low heat, stirring constantly. Cook, without stirring, until sugar is a deep caramel color, shaking pan frequently. Add remaining $\frac{1}{2}$ cup sugar and remaining 1 cup whipping cream. Cook, stirring occasionally, until a candy thermometer registers 210 degrees. Remove from heat. Stir in remaining 1 teaspoon vanilla and 1 tablespoon butter. Cool completely. Arrange pecan halves on top of cheesecake and serve with caramel sauce.

"When I'm invited to bring something for a potluck, this is the most requested dessert. I found this recipe in Southern Living many years ago - it's worth the work!"
Betty Rabin-Fung   **Sierra Vista Junior HS, Canyon Country, CA**

Awesome Texas Pecan Pie

Serves 6

> $\frac{1}{4}$ cup granulated sugar
> 1 cup white Karo syrup
> 2 teaspoons butter
> 2 eggs, beaten
> dash salt
> 1 teaspoon vanilla extract
> 1 cup pecans, shelled
> 1 9" unbaked pie shell

Preheat oven to 375 degrees. Combine sugar, syrup, butter, eggs, salt, vanilla and pecans. Pour into unbaked pie shell. Bake 50 to 60 minutes until filling doesn't shake when moved. Cool completely.

"This is the best made with Texas pecans you pick yourself!"

Dotti Jones   **Etiwanda High School, Rancho Cucamonga, CA**

Cherry Berry Ricotta Shortcake

Serves 8 - 10   *Photo opposite page 129*

Very Berry Sauce:
1 pint strawberries, cleaned, hulled, halved
$^1/_2$ pint raspberries
2 cups sweet cherries, pitted
$^3/_4$ cup sugar, or to desired sweetness
3 tablespoons Kirsch OR another liqueur (optional)
Shortcake:
2 cups all-purpose flour
1 tablespoon baking powder
2 tablespoons sugar
$^1/_2$ teaspoon salt
6 tablespoons unsalted butter, cut into pieces
1 cup Wisconsin Ricotta Cheese
$^2/_3$ cup milk
1 tablespoon sugar
sweetened whipped cream

Preheat oven to 425 degrees. *Prepare Sauce:* Combine fruits in a bowl. Toss with sugar and liqueur; set aside, stirring occasionally. *Prepare shortcake:* Sift flour, baking powder, sugar and salt together. Put in food processor work bowl, pulse several times. Add pieces of butter, whirl together 3 to 4 pulses. Add Ricotta cheese, pulse 5 to 6 times. With processor running, slowly add milk. Process about 5 seconds until ingredients are well combined. Turn out dough onto center of a baking sheet. Smooth into 8" flat circle. Form 3" hole in center of dough, making ring 2 $^1/_2$" thick. Sprinkle surface with 1 tablespoon sugar. Bake 20 to 25 minutes. Cool on baking sheet 20 minutes; remove to wire rack. Just before serving, slice shortcake in half horizontally with serrated knife. Remove top. Place bottom on large serving platter. Top with half the fruit. Place top of shortcake over fruit. Top with remaining fruit. Garnish with whipped cream.

"Shortcake ring can be made in advance and frozen."

Wisconsin Milk Marketing Board   **Madison, WI**

NOTES & REMINDERS

Banana Split Cake

Serves 12

1 cup margarine, divided
2 ¹/₂ cups powdered sugar, divided
2 cups graham cracker crumbs
2 egg whites
1 (15 ounce) can crushed pineapple, drained
3 bananas, sliced lengthwise
1 (large) container Cool Whip
¹/₂ cup almonds, sliced

Melt ¹/₂ cup margarine and combine with ¹/₂ cup powdered sugar and graham cracker crumbs; pat into bottom of a 9" x 13" pan. Beat together egg whites, ¹/₂ cup margarine and 2 cups powdered sugar. Pour over graham cracker crust. Spread pineapple over powdered sugar filling. Place sliced bananas on top of pineapple. Cover with Cool Whip and sprinkle with almonds. Refrigerate 2 hours.

Pat Smith   Kern Valley High School, Lake Isabella, CA

Chocolate Raspberry Terrine

Serves 8

Terrine:
8 ounces butter, unsalted
19 ounces semi-sweet chocolate
4 egg whites, beaten into soft peaks
1 cup heavy cream, beaten
¹/₈ cup sugar
3 (small) baskets raspberries
Glaze:
1 ¹/₂ pounds bittersweet chocolate
4 ounces butter, unsalted
2 cups heavy cream

Prepare terrine: Melt butter and semi-sweet chocolate in top of a double boiler. Fold in beaten egg whites, whipped cream and sugar. Layer half of this mixture into a loaf pan. Spread 2 baskets raspberries over chocolate layer. Top with remaining chocolate mixture. Spread evenly. Chill until firm.

Prepare glaze: Melt bittersweet chocolate, butter and heavy cream in top of double boiler. Cool until it becomes slightly thickened.

Assemble: Unmold terrine. Spread glaze evenly over terrine. Chill until chocolate is firm.

Serve: Slice remaining basket raspberries. Slice terrine and serve with sliced raspberries.

NOTE: Remaining raspberries can be pureed and strained to used as a sauce for terrine.

"This is a terrific make ahead dessert."

Betty Wells   **Bidwell Junior High School, Chico, CA**

Death by Chocolate

Serves 20

    1 (21.2 ounce) package brownie mix
    1/2 cup oil
    2 eggs
    1/4 cup water
    1/4 cup coffee flavored liqueur
        OR 4 tablespoons strong coffee with 1 teaspoon sugar
    3 packages chocolate instant pudding mix
    6 cups milk
    1/2 teaspoon almond extract
    1 (12 ounce) container non-dairy whipped topping
    1 package snack size chocolate covered toffee bars, crushed, divided

Preheat oven to 350 degrees. Prepare brownie mix with oil, eggs and water in a large bowl, according to package directions. Spread batter in pan and bake 24 to 26 minutes. Use wooden skewer to poke holes about 1" apart in top of warm brownies; drizzle with liqueur or coffee. Cool completely. Prepare pudding with milk in large bowl, according to package directions; set aside. In a medium bowl, fold almond extract into whipped topping; set aside. In a 4 quart serving bowl, break half of the brownies into bite-sized pieces. Sprinkle half of the crushed candies over brownies. Spread half of the pudding over candy pieces. Spread whipped topping over pudding. Repeat layers, ending with whipped topping. Cover and chill. Garnish with chocolate curls.

"A chocolate lover's dessert.
This dessert looks showy done in a clear glass footed serving bowl."

Millie Deeton   **Ayala High School, Chino Hills, CA**

Grandma's Easy Mock Eclair

Serves 8 - 12

    1 to 2 packages graham crackers
    1 (6 ounce) package instant vanilla pudding,
        prepared according to package directions
    9 ounces Cool Whip
    2 bananas, chopped, divided
    1 1/2 cups powdered sugar
    2 teaspoons corn syrup
    1/2 cup margarine
    4 teaspoons cocoa
    2 tablespoons hot milk

Line a 9" x 13" pan with graham crackers. Prepare instant pudding; fold Cool Whip into pudding. Pour 1/2 pudding over graham crackers. Sprinkle with 1 chopped banana. Spread pudding over the top to keep bananas from turning dark. Place another layer of graham crackers on top and repeat with bananas and pudding. Put a third layer of graham crackers on top. Using an electric mixer, beat together powdered sugar, corn syrup, margarine and cocoa. Beat in hot milk, 1 tablespoon at a time, until frosting is spreading consistency. Spread frosting on top of graham crackers, sealing all edges. Refrigerate 24 hours before serving.

"This is my son's favorite memory of his grandmother."

Bonnie Jakeway   **Rosemead High School, Rosemead, CA**

Orange Fluff

Serves 8

1 (6 ounce) package Orange Jell-O
1 (8 ounce) carton Cool Whip
1 (16 ounce) carton cottage cheese
1 (11 ounce) can mandarin oranges, drained
1 (6 ounce) can crushed pineapple, drained
chopped walnuts or sliced almonds

Mix dry jello with Cool whip and cottage cheese. Drain fruit and add it to the jello mixture. Gently fold together until fruit is distributed. Garnish with nuts. Chill at least 4 hours.

"Great for a potluck and easy to do ahead of time."

Laurie Paolozzi   **West High School, Torrance, CA**

Baked Apples with Cranberries & Maple Syrup

Serves 1

1 apple
1 tablespoon dried cranberries
1 tablespoon maple syrup
1 teaspoon butter

Wash one large apple for each person to be served. Remove core and place apple in baking dish. Fill the cored apple with cranberries, leaving space on top for butter. Drizzle maple syrup into hole and over top of apple. Place butter into top of hole. Cover with lid or foil. Bake at 350 degrees for 35 to 40 minutes.

"A dessert or a side dish with pork, beef, chicken. Help your family meet dietary guidelines for the recommended number of servings of fruits and vegetables."

Jackie Schaffer   **Morse High School, San Diego, CA**

Bananas Foster

Serves 4

$^1/_2$ stick butter (4 tablespoons)
1 cup brown sugar
2 bananas, sliced
2 ounces banana liqueur
4 ounces rum
ground cinnamon
vanilla ice cream

Melt butter in saucepan; add brown sugar and stir to form a creamy paste. Let mixture caramelize over medium heat for approximately 5 minutes. Stir in bananas, liqueur and rum. Heat and ignite carefully. Agitate to keep flame burning, add a few pinches cinnamon - voodoo magic - to flame. Let flame burn out and serve at once over ice cream.

"I learned how to make this at the New Orleans School of Cooking, while on vacation. A dramatic dessert to serve at an elegant dinner party."

Laura May   **Hesperia Junior High School, Hesperia, CA**

Grilled Peaches with Berry Sauce

Serves 6

$3/_4$ cup raspberries, in syrup
2 teaspoons lemon juice
3 medium peaches, peeled, halved
2 teaspoons brown sugar
$1/_2$ teaspoon cinnamon
$3/_4$ teaspoon vanilla
2 tablespoons butter or margarine

In a blender or food processor, puree raspberries and lemon juice; strain seeds. Cover and chill. Place peach halves, cut side up, on a piece of heavy duty foil. Combine brown sugar and cinnamon; sprinkle into peach centers. Sprinkle with vanilla. Dot with butter. Fold foil over peaches and grill over medium-hot coals for 10 to 15 minutes or until heated through. Spoon raspberry sauce over peaches and serve.

"This treat can be served with dinner, or you can use it as a dessert."

Robin Ali   **Nevada Union High School, Grass Valley, CA**

Strawberry Surprise

Serves 10 - 20

1 (large) container Cool Whip
1 quart strawberry yogurt
2 quarts fresh strawberries, washed, stems removed
5 kiwi fruit, peeled, cut into fourths
1 pineapple, peeled, cut into chunks
1 cantaloupe, peeled seeded, cut into chunks
1 (large) bunch grapes
2 bananas, peeled, cut into chunks

Combine Cool Whip with strawberry yogurt and stir until blended. Chill at least 1 hour. Meanwhile, prepare fruit, reserving a few strawberries for garnish. Place Cool Whip/yogurt dip in center of large platter. Arrange cut fruits around bowl and serve.

"Very good for summer parties!"

Carey H. Speer   **Las Vegas High School, Las Vegas, NV**

NOTES & REMINDERS

Buster Bar Dessert

Serves 8

> 1 (small) package Oreo cookies, crushed
> 1/4 cup margarine, melted
> 1/2 gallon vanilla ice cream
> 1 can hot fudge sauce
> 1 cup salted peanuts, crushed
> 1 (9 ounce) container Cool Whip

Combine crushed cookies with melted margarine; mix thoroughly. Reserve 1 cup and pack remaining mixture firmly into the bottom of a Tupperware container for cold cuts. Top with ice cream; freeze until firm. Pour 1 can hot fudge sauce over top. Sprinkle with nuts. Top with Cool Whip. Sprinkle reserved crumbs over top.

"So easy and so decadent!"

Joye Cantrell **Rialto High School, Rialto, CA**

Strawberry Daiquiri Dessert

Serves 8 - 12

> 1/4 cup margarine, melted
> 1 package graham crackers, crushed
> 1/4 cup sugar
> 1 can condensed milk
> 1 (large) package frozen strawberries, in syrup, thawed
> 1 can strawberry daiquiri concentrate (nonalcoholic)
> 1 (8 ounce) container Cool Whip

Toss margarine with graham crackers and sugar. Press into a 10" spring form pan to form a crust. Bake at 350 degrees for 10 minutes; cool. In a large mixing bowl, mix condensed milk with strawberries and daiquiri mix. Fold in Cool Whip. Pour over baked crust and freeze at least 4 hours. Take out of freezer about 15 minutes before serving. Garnish as desired.

"This is a beautiful, refreshing dessert. It goes well with Mexican foods."

Toni Purtill **Basic High School, Henderson, NV**

Tin Can Ice Cream

Serves 2

> 1 cup half & half, OR 1/2 cup milk + 1/2 cup whipping cream
> 1/4 cup sugar
> 1/4 teaspoon vanilla
> 2 tablespoons nuts or fruit, chopped
> 1 (1 pound) coffee can, with tight-fitting plastic lid
> 1 (3 pound) coffee can, with tight-fitting plastic lid
> crushed ice
> rock salt

Put half & half or milk with whipping cream, sugar, vanilla, and nuts or fruit in a 1 pound coffee can. Place lid on can. Place can inside a 3 pound can. Pack large can with crushed ice around smaller can. Pour at least $1/2$ cup rock salt evenly over ice. Place lid on 3 pound can. Roll back and forth on cement slab or table for 10 minutes. Open 3 pound can and remove 1 pound can. Stir contents of 1 pound can with rubber spatula, scraping sides of can. Replace lid. Drain ice water from larger can. Insert smaller can, pack with more ice and salt. Replace lid and roll back and forth 5 minutes more.

"This is easy and fun entertainment for a children's party."

Sue Walters   **Morse High School, San Diego, CA**

Vanilla Orange Delight
Serves 12

1 cup flour
$1/4$ cup brown sugar, firmly packed
$1/2$ cup nuts, chopped
$1/2$ cup margarine, melted
$1/2$ gallon vanilla ice cream, softened
1 quart orange sherbet, softened
4 cups whipped topping

Combine flour, brown sugar, nuts and margarine in bowl; mix well. Spread evenly in a 9" x 13" pan. Bake at 350 degrees for 15 minutes, stirring 3 times. Reserve $1/3$ cup crumbs. Press remaining crumbs into bottom of dish. Cool to room temperature. Layer vanilla ice cream, orange sherbet and whipped topping over crumb crust. Sprinkle with reserved crumbs. Freeze until serving time.

"This is cool and refreshing after a summer barbecue and can be done ahead. Yum!"

Penny Niadna   **Golden West High School, Visalia, CA**

Sherbet Watermelon
Serves 12 - 24

2 to 3 pints lime sherbet, softened
2 to 3 pints raspberry sherbet, softened
6 ounces chocolate chips

Line a round glass bowl with plastic wrap. Spoon softened lime sherbet around bottom and sides $3/4$" thick, smoothing as you go. Let harden in the freezer. Mix softened raspberry sherbet with chocolate chips and spoon inside lime sherbet rind. Freeze for $1 1/2$ hours. Unmold, remove plastic wrap and slice like a watermelon.

"Fun to make and tastes wonderful!"

Laura Giauque   **Olympus High School, Salt Lake City, UT**

Watermelon Ice

Serves 4 - 6

6 cups watermelon pieces, seeded
$1/2$ cup superfine sugar
2 tablespoons lemon juice, freshly squeezed

Puree watermelon pieces in 2 batches in a food processor or blender. Mix in sugar and lemon juice. Pour the puree into a plastic container or ice cube tray. Cover and freeze until almost set. Process watermelon ice again in food processor or blender until smooth. Repeat freezing and processing once more. Cover and freeze for about 3 hours or more, until ready to serve. Leave at room temperature for about 5 minutes before serving. Can also process in an ice cream maker.

"This is very refreshing and great for BBQ parties."

Patti Bartholomew   **Casa Roble High School, Orangevale, CA**

Contributors

A

Alfafara, Janet 69
Ontario HS, Ontario, CA

Ali, Robin. 143
Nevada City HS, Grass Valley, CA

Allen, Barbara 95
Ayala HS, Chino Hills, CA

Anagnos, Maridel 137
Tokay HS, Lodi, CA

Anderson, Marion S. 129
A.G.Currie MS, Tustin, CA

Aschenbrenner, Liz. 97
Sierra HS, Manteca, CA

Atkinson, Jeanette 131
Brinley MS, Las Vegas, NV

B

Baczynski, Kathie 114
Mt. Carmel HS, Poway, CA

Baker, Donna 128
Redlands East Valley HS, Redlands, CA

Ballard, Sue 52
Silverado HS, Victorville, CA

Barnes, Wendy 73
Vasquez HS, Acton, CA

Bartholomew, Patti 109, 146
Casa Roble HS, Orangevale, CA

Birch, Audrey 23
Parras MS, Redondo Beach, CA

Bitner, LeeAnn 48
Alta HS, Sandy, UT

Blanchette, Monica 26
Landmark MS, Moreno Valley, CA

Blohm, Rita 96
Nogales HS, La Puente, CA

Blough, Shirley. 136
Hillside MS, Simi Valley, CA

Bonilla, Pam. 44
Valley View HS, Moreno Valley, CA

Borden Foods Corp. 83
Columbus, OH

Bowman, Cindy. 125
McFarland HS, McFarland, CA

Brayton, Linda. 104
Grace Davis HS, Modesto, CA

Brokaw, Janis. 112
Mountain Shadows MS, Rohnert Pk, CA

Brown, Darlene V. 124
Golden Valley MS, San Bernardino, CA

Buchanan, Sherri. 23
Villa Park HS, Villa Park, CA

Burke, Brenda. 27
Mt. Whitney HS, Visalia, CA

Burkhart, Nanci. 58
Hueneme HS, Oxnard, CA

Burnham, Jill 37
Bloomington HS, Bloomington, CA

Burns, Priscilla. 108
Pleasant Valley HS, Chico, CA

C

Cahill, Pam 64
Eureka HS, Eureka, CA

Call, Carole. 15
Costa Mesa HS, Costa Mesa, CA

Campbell, Sue. 110

NOTES & REMINDERS

NOTES & REMINDERS

NOTES & REMINDERS

NOTES & REMINDERS

S

NOTES & REMINDERS

Recipes

NOTES & REMINDERS

NOTES & REMINDERS

NOTES & REMINDERS

NOTES & REMINDERS

157

NOTES & REMINDERS

For additional copies of *this* book,
and our *other* cookbook titles,
please visit our website:

www.CreativeCookbook.com

NOTES & REMINDERS